The Young Belloc

THE YOUNG HILAIRE BELLOC

BY

MARIE BELLOC LOWNDES

Author of

"THE LODGER," "I, TOO, HAVE LIVED IN ARCADIA,"
"WHERE LOVE AND FRIENDSHIP DWELT"
ETC. ETC.

P. J. KENEDY & SONS
NEW YORK

11,601

LIBRARY OF CONGRESS CATALOG CARD NUMBER: 56–5746
© 1956 BY P. J. KENEDY & SONS
PRINTED IN THE UNITED STATES OF AMERICA

FOREWORD

꘏꘏꘏

AFTER my mother, Mrs. Belloc Lowndes, had finished her four books of memoirs and family history, she found so much material for this book that she at once began to write it. She wrote the early chapters, and left many drafts of much of the book. The later chapters, which were not complete, have had letters added. But these letters my mother had herself put aside to weave into the story. She called it, in her own mind, "some records of youth and early middle age."

It is in no sense a biography of my uncle, Hilaire Belloc. Many parts of his life, especially his political career, and certain aspects of his writings, notably his historical and controversial studies, are hardly touched on at all. It sketches a relationship between people who loved each other, and it shows the early influences which contributed to the making of the man and the poet.

I wish to thank my uncle's children for their kindness in allowing me to quote letters from their mother. Also I thank Hilaire Belloc's literary executors (the Honorable Mrs. Raymond Asquith, the Right Reverend Monsignor Ronald Knox, and the late Viscount Norwich) for allowing me to publish the letters and early poems. Lastly I thank two writers, Susan Lowndes Marques and Mrs. Bernard Wall, for their suggestions and help.

ELIZABETH IDDESLEIGH

Pynes, Exeter

FAMILY TREE

[SHOWING HILAIRE'S PARENTAGE]

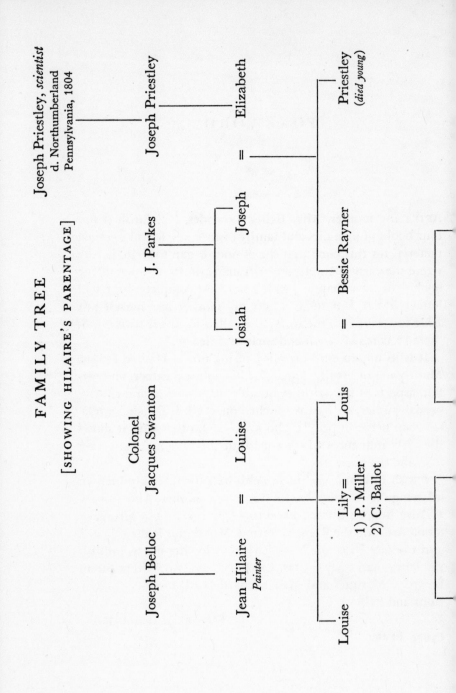

Joseph Priestley, *scientist*
d. Northumberland
Pennsylvania, 1804

Joseph Belloc

Jean Hilaire
Painter

Colonel
Jacques Swanton

Joseph Priestley

J. Parkes

Elizabeth

Josiah   Joseph

Louise

Louise

Lily =
1) P. Miller
2) C. Ballot

Louis

=

Bessie Rayner

Priestley
(*died young*)

CONTENTS

‣‣‣‣‣‣

THE YOUNG
HILAIRE BELLOC

1

THE FRENCH BACKGROUND

→»«←

I N A SMALL French engagement book for the year 1870, belonging to my mother and bound in what is now tattered
brown-watered silk, I see written in my father's hand on the
page for *"Mercredi, 27 Juillet: C'est aujourdh'ui à 4 h. ¼
qu'est né un beau gros garçon que je nommerai Joseph
Hilaire Pierre."*

The day of Hilaire Belloc's birth was intensely hot and
the weather broke with a terrific thunderstorm. Miss Mercy
Baker, a Quaker midwife who had come from London to
our French home wrote to one of my mother's friends: "It
is a moment of great rejoicing here, on account of the birth
of Madame Louis' little son. I was alone, and I brought the
baby into the world. The doctor, called by the astonishing
name of Mr. de Borgia, did not arrive until the event was
quite over, and the baby washed and dressed. The little fellow has done nothing but sleep since his advent, and his
mother has been reading the newspaper all the afternoon, so
you will judge how well she is. . . ."

Hilaire was born in the department of Seine-et-Oise near
Paris, in a beautiful village called La Celle Saint Cloud.
Our mother told me that when she married in the autumn of

1867 the village was composed of nothing but pre-revolution houses. La Celle is five miles from Saint-Germain, on the edge of the splendid woods which stretch out to Versailles, and is situated on a high hill above the Seine.

Hilaire's birth took place in what was called *le grand salon* of his father's house. This was an airy pleasant drawing-room with a white rose-wreathed balcony whence wooden steps led down to the garden. The room had been turned into a bed-room for the occasion. A door from the drawing-room led into a lobby where a corkscrew staircase led up to three bed-rooms and a dressing-room. These rooms were given over to Hilaire and myself during my father's lifetime, as he and my mother always slept next door in what was called the Châlet.

I was two years old when my brother was born.

The romantic marriage of my parents, Louis Belloc and Bessie Parkes, the terrible events which took place in the War of 1870, and the early death of my father, were described in my book *I, Too, Have Lived in Arcadia*, so I shall only touch on these matters here.

Hilaire's father, Louis Belloc, was a member of the French bar, but he had become an invalid at the age of twenty-eight as a result of a serious illness. He was the only son of Hilaire Belloc, the painter, and of Louise Swanton, the youngest daughter of Jacques Swanton, one of the last colonels of the Berwick Regiment. Hilaire and Louise Belloc had two daughters, Louise and Lily, who were both older than my father.

Madame Swanton Belloc was now a widow; her husband had died shortly before my parents' marriage. She left La Celle Saint Cloud together with her lifelong friend, Made-moiselle de Montgolfier, to stay with her elder daughter Louise, in a beautiful and historic house called Villebouzin, so that my father and mother would have the house at La Celle to themselves.

My mother wrote the following account of her mother-in-law, our beloved grandmother Belloc: "In recording the bare details of that long life I hardly know how to express the affection and reverence with which I regarded my husband's mother. She was the noblest human being I have ever known.

"She had met almost all the outstanding people in the intellectual and literary worlds in France and in England. She had known well, in her own country, Lamartine, Michelet, and, in 1824, Stendhal had written the preface to a life she wrote of Lord Byron. She also knew Thiers, Guziot, and Victor Hugo. She was the first writer to translate Dickens into French, and her translation of *Uncle Tom's Cabin* was still in print in 1914. Among her English friends were people as different as Maria Edgeworth, Tom Moore, and, in later years, Lady Byron.

"In her old age she lamented that she had never known George Sand, whose autobiography, full of mature wisdom, filled her with admiration. Attempts had been made during that long life to bring them together, but Madame Belloc once said to me, 'I would gladly have known her, but I did not think it compatible with my duty to my daughters.' She would have rejoiced, had she lived, to know that Nohant had become the property of the French Government.

"She spoke the two languages to perfection, but her English, though fluent and correct, might be termed majestic. When she took up a newspaper or a book to read out loud to me, I never knew in which language she was speaking, her meaning seemed to come direct in all its fullness without the intervention of words. She was a fervent Christian and a practising Catholic."

Hilaire Belloc's mother was English; her name was Bessie Rayner Parkes, and she was a Warwickshire woman, a descendant of Joseph Priestley, the scientist who discovered oxygen and invented soda-water. Priestley took refuge in New England after the Tory mob had burnt his house in Birmingham. The pretext for this destruction was that he had been present at a banquet held to commemorate the fall of the Bastille. As a matter of fact, he had not attended the banquet, but he did undoubtedly sympathize with the aims of the Revolution. His little granddaughter Eliza Priestley, Bessie's mother, came back to England with her family as a child. She married Joseph Parkes in 1824.

In the spring of 1867 my mother, Bessie Rayner Parkes (to whom I shall usually refer throughout my story as Bessie, as she was known to her many friends), together with her friend Barbara Bodichon, took for a few weeks a small chalet which was in the garden of the house where Louise Swanton Belloc was then living with her son, Louis.

Louis and Bessie became engaged within a few weeks of their first meeting. But both Bessie's circle in England and Louis' family at La Celle Saint Cloud felt grave fears for their future happiness. Bessie had led an active, interesting life in London, and was already in her thirties. Though she spoke French well, she had seen little of French family life. Louis' physical condition appeared far worse than it really was, especially to those who were not closely acquainted with him. He was slightly lame and extremely silent and reserved in manner. His mother thought it only right that before he considered marriage he should consult a leading Paris specialist. The letter his mother subsequently wrote to Bessie in England must have appeared a terrible verdict, for, in the specialist's considered opinion, Louis Belloc ought never to marry, if only because, apart from everything else, he was not likely to have children.

Bessie answered that letter by stating that children had never seemed to her of particular importance in married life, and she intended to keep her word and marry Louis, if he was of the same mind. Their wedding took place in London on September 19th, 1867, in the old Embassy Church of St. James, Spanish Place.

My mother looked many years younger than her age. She was a little below medium height; she was slight as a young woman, with a clear complexion and very little colour. Her one beauty lay in bright auburn naturally wavy hair, and she had a beautiful speaking voice. She was always indifferent to what happened to be the fashion of the day. At a time when brilliant colours were being worn she preferred neutral tints; greys and delicate shades of blue.

When my parents first met, Bessie had been a Catholic for two years, having been received into the Church in 1865 by Monsignor Gilbert in St. Mary's, Moorfields. She had been born into a Unitarian circle, and she retained all her life a respect and affection for those holding this creed. Still she had never regarded herself as belonging in any real sense to that body. Very early in life she became a high-minded free-thinker and it was only gradually that she came to accept the claims of the Catholic Church. Before being received she had attended Mass every Sunday for nine years.

In one of her now forgotten books called *In a Walled Garden,* she tells something of her conversion. "Somebody, I forget whom, who saw that I was tending to the Church, urged me to go and see Dr. Manning, and I remember feeling a strong disinclination to do so. I had never spoken to any human being, priest or pastor, on spiritual things; but an ap-

pointment was made with him. I was shown into a small, narrow room, where I waited a few minutes, and then the tall,
thin, severe-looking priest came in. He was not severe in later
years and, to one who knew him well and loved him much,
it is not easy to accurately record that first impression. He was
perfectly polite, but I thought that he disliked speaking to a
woman who had taken an active part in a public movement
[the movement for Women's Rights]. This may have been a
morbid impression on my part, but it caused me to be frightened. I was not long in the room, but though he spoke with
the most measured chilly calmness, the few things he said
made a deep and lasting effect on me. He told me that 'by the
mercy of God' he had never doubted of His Personality. He
spoke as if perfectly conscious of the Comtist influence then
taking possession of English society. It was just at the time
when George Henry Lewes and George Eliot were beginning
to reign supreme.

"If one so peculiarly impersonal as Dr. Manning could
stoop to a personal revelation, the words and the accent he
used may be held to have conveyed this meaning: 'Though I
am well aware of the length to which the controversy has been
carried, still I have never had to concern myself with it. Doubt
never touched me in that direction. I have always had an entire faith in a Personal God.' He advised me to read up the
history of the Reformation on all sides, for which he put
down several books on a sheet of paper, and among them
D'Aubigné, remarking calmly, 'but it is full of lies.' In this
interview Dr. Manning gave me no spiritual advice, made no
appeal to me. I do not think he had any suspicion that I was
so impressed and overpowered by his intellect that when I
left the room and the house I ran nearly all the way home,
with the sense that I was fleeing from an overmastering
brain."

On another occasion she wrote: "It is not in the least true that I embraced Catholicism as a defence against scepticism. So far as my personal life is concerned I should have been extremely happy and comfortable in a sceptical state, except when just under the immediate presence of trouble. . . .

"If there were no future life, I should still consider the years I have had of mortal life a most precious gift of the Supreme Creative Power. On every side I see pain and want, and I have always been haunted by the misery of the world. It was really and truly this, and this only, that gradually brought me into the Christian Fold; and it was the active, ordered charity of the Catholic Church which made me captive.

"I do not take any personal interest in the emotional side of religion. Neither St. Teresa nor Mrs. Pearsall Smith touch me in my inner self. The appeal is to emotions I never experienced, to wants I never felt. Often I blame myself for this incapacity. I see that other people in all ages are profoundly moved by feelings which to me are a sealed book. I love my fellow-creatures not only *en particulier* but also *en gros,* because I understand what they suffer. And I am strongly attached to Catholic worship in the service of the Mass. And in the upper chambers of my mind I have a strong grip of the Creed—the doctrine of Hell apart, of which I have not a strong grip at all, thinking silently that here there is some unexplained mystery."

Some people thought, and it has appeared in print, that Bessie became a Catholic when she married Louis—a misapprehension that irritated her family intensely. That is why I have dwelt on her conversion and her feelings towards the Church—as well as because she was the greatest single influence in Hilaire's early life. Her marriage, in the face of opposition, merely confirmed her religious beliefs: "My mar-

riage, and all that was said and written by those who loved me
at that time, or perhaps I ought to say before my marriage,
cured me of any tendency to look at anything but the very
central principle of all. See how the results in all ways belied
everybody's prophecies and fears, and how the truth of the
religious root blossomed out, and brought all the prophets to
nought, though they all brought to bear the best intentions
in what they said and wrote."

The birth of a son gave intense joy to our grandmother
Belloc. She had ardently wished that Louis should have a son,
and that he should be called Hilaire after her husband. A
family tradition concerning our painter grandfather, and one
which delighted Hilaire, was that he had been taken as a child
to Paris in the middle of the Revolution to consult a doctor,
and the man-servant they had brought with them took him to
the window so that he could see Danton on his way to the scaf-
fold.

From early in July, 1870, ominous rumours of approaching
war with Prussia came to La Celle Saint Cloud. Our English
grandmother Parkes wrote imploring Bessie to bring herself
and the children to England. Bessie had made a quick re-
covery from Hilaire's birth and agreed to travel as soon as
Mercy Baker thought it would be safe. Meanwhile it was arranged that Hilaire should be baptized *dans l'intimité*. He
was given the names *Jean Hilaire* after his French grandfather, *Joseph* after his English grandfather, and *Pierre* after
my father's favourite cousin who was dead. My first cousin
who was also my godfather, René Millet, eldest son of my
father's sister Lily, was present, and already in uniform.

At that time there was no thought of the German army
reaching Paris, and anyway Bessie believed that any Germans
penetrating into France would behave well and in a civilized

way. She had often stayed in Germany as a girl with the de Bunsens, had a veneration for Goethe and had paid two visits to Weimar. Her optimism, however, was not shared either by my grandmother Belloc or by Adelaide de Montgolfier.

On August 25th, 1870, Bessie wrote to her English uncle Josiah Parkes: "I got your letter yesterday and hasten to assure you that we are all well and safe and the Prussians as yet nowhere near Paris. Louis has gone into town today to get our passports signed. We can then get across country any day to the Rouen and Le Havre railway, without going near Paris. . . . Little Mary is very well and bonny. Little Joseph Hilary is very plump and good, sleeping the greater part of the time. I have recovered remarkably well. The only way in which the war could affect Louis personally is that we fear this hill may be occupied *should* the Prussians approach Paris; and we have a house full of pictures and books and should not like it burnt. But we must hope for the best, and that they won't come. I write shortly being very much occupied with the baby. The English nurse who was to have come yesterday from London did not appear. I cannot imagine where she is! And meanwhile I have the little man on my hands day and night."

If she had to leave La Celle, Bessie would have liked to go, at least for a while, to her and Louis' apartment in Paris in the Rue de Vaugirard whence she had written a few months earlier: "Our rooms are near the famous old Luxembourg Garden and to our great delight two private pieces of ground close to the palace have been thrown open to the public, and very prettily planted in the English style. The rest is all as it was, wide walks and statues, with a large round basin in the centre. Mary goes there every day to walk in company with hundreds of other babies. She runs about like a happy kitten and is as strong and hearty as possible."

Had Bessie stayed in this apartment that she loved so much, Hilaire would certainly not have lived, for almost every child under three died during the siege of Paris and Hilaire was very delicate during his infancy and early childhood. Luckily wiser counsels prevailed. As it was, my grandmother Belloc had already left France and taken refuge with a daughter in Richmond, England, before Louis and Bessie took the keys of their house at La Celle to the *mairie,* and with their tiny children, travelled by the last train that left Paris for Dieppe. As the train steamed out of the station men shovelled earth over the rails behind it.

Adelaide de Montgolfier was eighty-one, but she refused to leave Paris and remained there all through the siege. Bessie wrote some years later: "No biography of this very distinguished Frenchwoman [she was the daughter of Etienne de Montgolfier who invented the balloon] has appeared, except a paragraph in a great dictionary recording her few books by their titles. She was the only person whom I ever heard speak of the French revolution as an eye-witness. This aged lady, who was the closest friend of our family, was born in 1789 and lived to be ninety. She was therefore four years old at the time of the death of Marie Antoinette, but as she lived not in Paris but at Annonay near Lyons, her most distinct memory was that of being awakened by men with torches in the middle of the night: men who came searching under her little bed for a hunted priest."

Hilaire was just over a month old when we reached England.

My English grandmother Parkes would have liked the whole party to come to her, but as we had brought with us two excellent French maids, Ada and Adeline, Bessie accepted the offer of a little house in Great College Street, Westminster, belonging to her uncle Josiah. Though the house was small we all managed to pack in, and it was there that my parents, Hilaire and I spent the winter of 1870.

Bessie had always been deeply attached to her uncle Josiah. When young he had made an unhappy marriage, and though his wife had soon died, he never married again. He was very fond of his sister-in-law, our grandmother Parkes, and a letter from her to him in later life says: " 'Though I do not suppose you are aware of it, you and I have known each other exactly sixty years. I found an allusion to my first meeting you and my dear husband in a letter written by my father. What nice clever boys you both were!''

Josiah on his side was extremely fond of Bessie, and proud of her. He accepted both her change of religion and her marriage to a delicate Frenchman with philosophical detachment. He was pleased when I was born, but more pleased still at Hilaire's birth and he insisted on seeing him naked so as to ascertain that he was without blemish. In his letters to his sister-in-law and his niece he never failed to inquire after the children. It pleased him in a quiet way to know that they would in time inherit the money he had made with so much hard work. He lived to be nearly eighty years old, dying in August, 1871.

Though now surrounded by her loving English relations, Bessie was thinking all the time of France, as her letters show. Writing from the little house in Westminster she says: "We *live* on the newspapers; and are very anxious, as you may suppose. I would give the world to be at La Celle. Even in the midst of the Prussians!"

That winter held many dark and indeed miserable days for Bessie. She was aware that her husband was extremely unhappy, though he remained very silent as to what he was feeling, and she must have known also that Madame Belloc felt something like despair. She had not lived with her elder daughter Louise for many years, and she found life at Richmond, though surrounded not only with comfort but with luxury, intolerably trying, for the mother and daughter had hardly anything in common excepting their love of reading. They heard from Paris constantly, but it soon became clear to them that no letters got through from England.

"Great College Street, 12th Feb., 1871. . . . We have had a letter from Paris dated Feb. 4th. No mention of *starvation;* only the usual horseflesh had given out, and my brother-in-law's pretty carriage horses were taken that very day though he tried to buy them off. He speaks of the family as well, and Mademoiselle de Montgolfier in a terrible state of *guerre à l'outrance.* It is a bitter pill for her to swallow in her proud historical old age. Mrs. Westlake told me yesterday that Lord Granville told Mr. Townsend that the Prussians had bought up all the ordnance maps of the south of England. A nice prospect! Imagine Bexhill 'requisitioned' and a Prussian regiment billetted on Robertsbridge; and 2 Uhlans riding up to Brightling Rectory; and Ben and Gillett shot down for resisting them and protecting the Misses Hayles! I told Mrs. Westlake it was all of a piece with the gobbling up of Hanover and Frankfurt. But she seemed to think the public benefit to Germany excused *that.* Surely the little old States and universities were far more conducive to freedom? I have a curious report on Trades Unions to review for the *Spectator.* Much about Holland. It will be a sad pity if Holland is gobbled up also. Mr. Edgeworth spoke the other day as if they might 'reasonably want' a part of it. As for that, Dover and Portsmouth would of course be useful to them, as they are short of sea ports."

On March 30th, at the time of the Commune, Bessie wrote to her uncle Josiah: "You kindly enquire about our Paris friends and relations. They seem to be well, though my brother-in-law, Charles Ballot, was in the procession upon which the mob fired a week ago. I have written urging his wife to come to London with their little Marcel who is ten years old, but she will not leave her husband and he says that if all the party of order run away there will be no hope of restoration of a good government. Some people hope that the insurgents will very soon be short of money, but I am afraid that they may then take to organized pillage requiring all citizens to give up their money and valuables."

Bessie insisted on returning to La Celle in May 1871, as soon as possible after the end of the Commune. During the war the house had been reduced to little more than a shell. Sixty German soldiers and one officer had been quartered there, a change of officer and men taking place every fortnight. Great mounds of books, papers and letters were piled up in the garden and in the little field which formed part of the property. Only a few of their possessions survived: a man in the village to whom Louis had been kind had gone into the house soon after the war began and had taken four family pictures out of their frames, rolled them up and hidden them.

Louis and Bessie were spared seeing the house in the state in which it had been left by the Prussians, for before they came my two French aunts had done all they could to make the house once more possible as a habitation. The walls had been washed and furniture of a kind, and in spite of the shortage, had been installed. All through our childhood there were only lining-papers in most of the rooms, and years went by before ordinary wall-papers were put up in the bedrooms. But Bessie was determined that at least the *grand salon* should look a little as it had looked at the time of her marriage. I found not long ago an envelope in which were small pieces of red paper, and on it was written: "The patterns of wall-paper looked at by Louis and me for the *grand salon*." But the house was never the same, and Bessie used often to describe to me how beautiful the rooms had been, how fine the furniture, how delightful the books, pictures and miniatures.

One of the pictures which was saved was a portrait of my great-uncle Armand Swanton, painted in his uniform as one of Napoleon's aides-de-camp. It is now in Hilaire's English home in Sussex, but during our childhood it hung in the *grand salon* at La Celle, forming a curious pendant to a portrait of Armand Swanton's sister, Caroline, who had become a nun in 1814.

In the autumn following my birth, Grandmother Belloc had gone to Metz where this sister, Soeur Saint Julienne, was dying. Our aunt, Louise Redelsperger, had nursed her devotedly for some weeks, and with the extraordinary energy which characterized her, she actually painted this large picture of her aunt. It is a remarkable picture, and my aunt painted a copy of it which I believe still hangs in the convent of which Soeur Sainte Julienne had become Mother Superior after having been fifty years in religion.

Apropos of this family bereavement Bessie wrote: "Madame Belloc feels it excessively. The nun had always kept up the warmest relations with her sisters and their children. At the time of her religious Jubilee in 1864 she was actually allowed to come to Paris with another religious and stay with the Hilaire Bellocs for a whole month." Soeur Sainte Julienne returned to her convent at Metz, and she died at eighty years of age, before the entry of the German troops in 1870.

It was always thought by my grandmother Belloc that her saintly sister Caroline had exercised a powerful influence upon the mind of her husband Jean Hilaire, the artist. Born in revolutionary times, his baptism had left no record, but a year before his death he became a convinced Catholic, and was in close communion with a remarkable curé at St. Sulpice.

On July 28th, 1871, when Hilaire was just one, my grandmother Parkes wrote to Uncle Josiah: "Bessie and the children are now settled in her little house at La Celle St. Cloud. It is, I trust, tolerably repaired. She writes they go about to the neighbouring villages and hear many interesting things from the people there. She is in despair as to French politics and is particularly horrified at the dissensions in the Assembly. She gives good accounts of the children. Little Marie is so happy at being home, busy making jam with a kitchen towel round her waist. The boy is very placid, and I hope he will steady her as time goes on. She is so high-spirited, not easy to manage. I hope the boy when he can talk will take her down, but if he does, his work will be cut out, for she is sturdy and self-willed, liking her way—as who does not?"

Louis and Bessie travelled constantly between France and England. On one occasion, after arriving at La Celle from England, Bessie wrote to her mother: ". . . Our wanderings are ended; we got here at seven on Saturday, with ten packages registered by railway to say nothing of the babies and the handbags. I am not sorry to have no more moving at present. Now I am back from Paris where I have been all day with Madame Belloc. I found my boxes at the Gare du Nord; and glad I was to see their familiar brown faces behind a great modern cage. One was full of Cawthorne & Hutt's books—all my intellectual food for weeks. The other was full of things for the babies—paints, a pack of cards for 'Beggar my Neighbour,' prints to colour, all laid in at Meyers' in Berners Street. And a great unpacking did we have tonight before I got them off to bed; and then Mary nearly went to sleep over her prayers. I walked up from the Seine, following Maman and the little donkey carriage piled up with luggage; and then after dinner I sat on the floor and devoted myself wholly to the babies and the teetotums, and so my physical energies have nearly come to an end."

There followed a month later: "Hilaire is promoted to meals at table with his little silver *couvert* which Uncle Josiah gave him, and his Papa's college cup. He behaves well, which is saying something for not quite 22 months old. He brandishes his blunt silver knife which he calls a Toto."

Hilaire's second birthday, on July 27th, 1872, was celebrated in the English way by Bessie. She wrote her mother a happy account of the day, and added that she and my father were going off on a little tour in provincial France. Even in extreme old age—and she lived to be ninety-five—she never liked staying for long in one place.

Louis, who may truly be said to have adored her was always willing to do whatsoever she wished—so he consented to leave his cool comfortable house in the torrid heat of summer. That year in early August, just after my fourth birthday, one of Bessie's American Priestley cousins, who was in Europe, wanted to visit Auvergne, so my mother decided that she and my father would join him there. She knew nothing of that part of France, so though she was warned that it would be very hot, they went off and she and my father joined Mr. Priestley.

One day, while they were on this trip my father stood at midday with his head bare, as a long funeral procession went by. Later he complained of feeling very tired, and Bessie, who always took sudden decisions, made up her mind that they would come home a few days earlier than they had intended.

When they arrived at La Celle Saint Cloud Louis, still feeling great fatigue, did not dine with the others in *la grande maison,* but went straight to bed next door in the little house called the Châlet, where he and Bessie lived. The Châlet had only two good bedrooms, the one was occupied by Louis, the other by Bessie; there was a tiny dressing-room between the two rooms, and the bath-room was on the ground floor. There every morning Bessie took a cold bath, to the astonishment and dismay of her French relations.

The evening of their return Bessie dined as usual with my grandmother Belloc and Mademoiselle de Montgolfier, and described to them the delightful tour she and Louis had made. After dinner Mademoiselle de Montgolfier went next door to see Louis, but came back to say that he was asleep—she was worried for it was odd that he had gone to sleep so soon.

The next morning, when Bessie went to visit Louis in his bedroom, she found that he was still fast asleep. She felt a little, but not very anxious, as once before he had slept for twenty-four hours and waked up refreshed and perfectly well. After luncheon it was Mademoiselle de Montgolfier who went again to the Châlet. She came back and asked Bessie to send for the doctor as she had not been able to wake Louis. This Bessie refused to do as she knew it would irritate her husband. Then my grandmother went to see Louis, and felt so alarmed at his condition that on her own responsibility she sent a note to the village doctor asking him to come as soon as possible.

Towards evening Mademoiselle de Montgolfier wrote a long letter to a dutiful nephew. In it she described little Hilaire, saying "he is very unlike what his father was at his age, for Louis was a beautiful child. Hilaire is almost ludicrously like his grandfather, after whom he was named," and she goes on to hope that he, too, will be a painter. She ends by saying that she is leaving the envelope open as she hopes to persuade Louis, though not well, to write a few words about the tour from which he and Bessie have just returned. This letter was never sent.

About an hour later Mademoiselle de Montgolfier went to the Châlet where she found the tiny drawing-room and dining-room in darkness. The light of a candle came from Louis' room. She went upstairs, crept into the room and sat by my grandmother in dumb anguish. The village doctor was there, having been taken up by Bessie. After a brief examination he looked at her and said: "*Il passe.*" Bessie thought he meant that the *malaise* was "passing." The doctor and my grandmother left the room together. On her return my grandmother told Bessie that she must send for the priest, so my mother decided to go for him herself.

The old priest came at once accompanied by an acolyte and bringing the Blessed Sacrament. He found that Louis could not speak, so he only anointed him. Then he led Bessie out onto the balcony and told her she must call on all her courage as her husband was dying and would probably remain unconscious to the end. Those present knelt down while the Abbé de Boncourt recited the prayers for the dying. Bessie held Louis in her arms with his head resting on her breast for five hours. It was just after eleven o'clock when he ceased to breathe.

Louis died so quietly that Bessie would not have known he was dead had not Mademoiselle de Montgolfier, who was his godmother, gone into convulsions of grief. My grandmother led her into the house next door. When she returned she found her daughter-in-law sitting by the bed, composed and tearless, writing a letter to her mother.

"My dearest Mother, a dreadful blow has fallen on me. Louis is dead. The heat and fatigue of the voyage to Auvergne caused his death. But he wished to go. The doctor says he would have always been liable to what is called an *insolation.* . . . You know my Louis was the kindest and best husband a woman ever had. I will come to you when I can do so. I feel quite well, so do not be anxious about me."

Our grandmother hoped Bessie would spend the rest of the night with her two children. But she refused to do so, preferring to stay in her own bedroom. I vividly remember being taken with Hilaire into my father's room. He looked as if he was asleep. We were told to kiss his hand, and we were then taken away.

The next morning Bessie added the following words to the letter to her mother: "Madame Belloc is dreadfully distressed though she retains complete command of herself. Little Marie evidently knows something is wrong, for she cries sadly. Poor little Hilaire is too young to know what his loss will mean to him. Please don't make yourself ill in grieving over me, or I shall not know where to turn for comfort. You have always been so strong, and have always comforted me." Her letter was dated August 20th, 1872.

The next day Bessie again wrote to her mother. "The funeral will be tomorrow, so quick is it in France. Lily and Charles, who have just arrived, assure me that our journey to Auvergne had little or nothing to do with Louis' death. But it stupifies me to think that after these five years of what I can truly call boundless personal devotion, I should have been the person to lead him into possible danger. But no one had ever told me that there was danger of cerebral congestion. My dearest mother, I know you feel for me. But no one knows, and no one will ever know, what he was to me, far more than my children, so good, so dear, so loving in domestic life."

On August 23rd, the day after our father's funeral, my aunt Lily insisted on taking Bessie to Paris to her apartment for a few days. From there my mother wrote: "I am returning to La Celle Saint Cloud tomorrow evening to dinner. Oh my dearest mother, I feel such a horror at the thought of going back. But it has to be done. I don't wish to give a feeling in the village that I ran away from my children or from the old ladies. . . . I had given up everything for Louis and I don't know how to take up a single thread of my life again. My marriage was to me the re-making of my life, and I seem to have done it so thoroughly and to have found the means of making not only myself, but everybody around me, happy. . . .

"Our little children both went to the funeral, poor little Hilaire going round with the *quête:* all I saw was the little man in his white and black frock led round the church. After everyone had left the cemetery, Marie and I threw flowers into the grave. I threw on to Louis' coffin a most beautiful red rose which seemed to me symbolic of the happy life of husband and of father that Louis had led. Will you have the kindness to put a notice in *The Times?* His age was forty-two, his name Louis Marie Belloc. Do you think you could add that he was the son-in-law of the late Joseph Parkes—my dear kind father? But, oh mother, I can't bear to write about it all for it seems so very terrible to me. Madame Belloc wants me to come to you some time next week, perhaps on Monday. But I must see how we all get on. I know that I am writing in a selfish way. I know that you feel the loss, for he had really become like a son to you, and when speaking of you he always did so in so wonderfully tender and thoughtful a way."

I clearly remember my father's funeral. Hilaire, who was two years and three weeks old, was chief mourner and held my mother's hand. I have no recollection of the requiem Mass, but I do remember the scene in our little cemetery. It was reached by a very steep and extremely rough path. A great number of years, indeed a lifetime, went by before that rough path was made smooth.

In my childhood, death was rarely mentioned in the presence of an English child. This was far from being the case in France. We were quite familiar with the thought of death, and from the time we could walk we were always present at the funerals of any of our friends who died in the village where we spent each summer. I must hasten to add that we also went to the village weddings and baptisms; these functions we much enjoyed.

Various English friends came to see my mother that autumn, each staying for a few days and all of them trying to comfort her. But nothing availed. It seemed as if a state of happiness would never return to her.

Throughout our childhood, my mother made a point of being in our French home on All Souls' Day. When she was over ninety she described to me that first All Souls' Day in 1872, a little more than two months after my father's death. It was a lovely autumn day, and after the requiem high Mass, we walked up to the cemetery with all the people present. To my mother it brought sharp agony, though she was moved by the piety with which everyone visited their own family grave. I remember that for certainly a full year after my father's death we wore either black or white clothes. We were quite often taken to the cemetery by various members of the family, but not by our mother except on All Souls' Day.

We used to kneel down and pray for our father's soul.

2

HILAIRE'S CHILDHOOD

→⟩⟨←

THE NEXT YEARS of Hilaire's and my life were divided fairly evenly between England and France. We both loved our French home dearly. We spoke French well, but at no point could we have been actually taken for French children—though Hilaire, as all his friends know, pronounced his r's in the French way.

Hilaire and I were extraordinarily different. Whereas he passed every examination with brilliant ease, I was unable to pass with credit even a very simple test. It was a tribute to Bessie's character that she never made me feel when we were children the intellectual disparity between Hilaire and myself. I took his maturity of mind for granted and never envied him in any way. Perhaps this was partly because I was the pet and darling of my grandmother Belloc, Mademoiselle de Montgolfier, and my two French aunts, Lily Ballot and Louise Redelsperger. I was very like my father, to whose memory they were all passionately devoted. Bessie loved me dearly but she did not understand my character, for I was entirely unlike any English child she had ever known. On the other hand Hilaire's remarkable and original mind—for such it showed itself to be from the day he began to speak plainly—delighted her, though she wisely did nothing to press him forward.

Soon after our father's death there was held a family council in which it was decided that Anatole Dunoyer de Ségonzac, a distinguished man who had been a friend of my father's in his youth, should be appointed our guardian, or *tuteur*. But in fact years went by before Monsieur Dunoyer played any part in Hilaire's or my life—not, indeed, until Hilaire suddenly decided that he would like not only to live in France but actually to join the French navy, when our guardian at once came forward and willingly consented to be his ward's guarantor at the Collège Stanislas, the old Catholic school in Paris where boys wishing to become naval officers were trained.

Grandmother Parkes persuaded Bessie to send our French nurse, Adeline, back to her home in Algiers, and to engage an old-fashioned English nurse. Thus there came into our lives Sarah Mew. Nurse Mew had a lifelong influence on Hilaire's character. While not specially caring for me, she soon became completely devoted to Hilaire. She came from a Methodist family but gave her word that she would make no effort to influence our religious views—indeed it would have been difficult to do so in Hilaire's case for it seemed as if he were "instinctively" Catholic.

In only one letter of Hilaire's, written at the age of seven in round childish writing, have I found a word which might be regarded as having been inspired by Nurse Mew. It was written at the time of grandmother Parkes' death in 1877: "My darling Mama, I am very sorry Grandmama is Dead and that I shall never see her again. I send you a text, God is love."

When she came to us Sarah Mew must have been about fifty, tall and stately in appearance—in her youth she certainly must have been beautiful. But she was a broken-hearted woman, for her previous charge, a little girl called Ethel whom she had brought up and whom she loved with the jeal-

ous devotion of a reserved nature, had been suddenly and in-
exorably sent to a boarding school, and Sarah Mew had been
given a month's notice. However, she soon managed to trans-
fer her love to Hilaire, and she loved him the more as he was
a delicate child.

Hilaire and I possessed two cats. Bessie allowed them to
travel with us to and fro between France and England. My
cat was called Josephine; she was pure white and had the most
beautiful blue eyes. Hilaire's was called Moonie. Nurse Mew
must have been a devoted cat-lover, as she never made any
difficulties about the cats but accepted them as part of her
new life. I have a letter from her in which she says: "I know
you are pleased that dear old Josephine had some more kit-
tens, she will be more amiable now. . . ." And yet things
were never the same for me after the arrival of Nurse Mew.
But, as seems usual with children, it never occurred to me to
allow my mother to know how great a change the arrival of
Nurse had made. When in our French home, to Nurse's
strong disapproval, I spent the whole of the day either in the
drawing-room or in the garden.

Our garden at La Celle was filled with mystery and delight
as was the large meadow beyond which we called *le pré,*
where, after I could read, I spent some of my happiest hours.
The meadow lay between a little-frequented steep road, and
the highway to Bougival. Between the meadow and the road
was a narrow wood which both Hilaire and I loved, especially
in spring when it was full of wild lilies-of-the-valley, bluebells,
primroses and wind-flowers. We were constantly with Mademoiselle de Montgolfier, whom we called "Maman Aïde."
She wandered about the house and garden like a delicate
wraith. Now close on ninety, her memory had completely
gone. She was aware of this fact, and therefore spoke very

little, never saying anything which could have made her seem strange or different from those about her. She took little notice of Hilaire, but concentrated her attention on me. I do not remember feeling surprised or distressed by "Maman Aïde's" condition. She was so completely a part of the texture of our daily life, and there was nothing peculiar in her appearance.

From what most people would call infancy we always went to Mass on Sunday, and I can truly say that we thoroughly enjoyed doing so. Every now and then it was my turn to carry round a basket nearly as large as myself filled with pieces of *pain béni,* which was in reality that most delicious cake called *brioche.* There had been a medieval church at La Celle Saint Cloud, but it was destroyed during the Revolution by a mob streaming out from Versailles. In its place had been built a singularly ugly edifice dearer to me than any other church in the world.

There was a village choir. The sermon never lasted more than ten minutes and was well suited to a childish mind, being simple and practical. Hilaire delighted in any kind of sermon. What I enjoyed was the music and the pleasant knowledge that after Mass we would meet all our friends outside the church on the Place. I can just remember the Abbé de Boncourt who had been summoned so suddenly when my father was dying. He was a very cultivated old man who lived a life of austerity in his plain clergy-house, though he sometimes came to play whist with my grandmother. She must have made a great difference to his life as she lent him all the new books.

The Fourteenth of July is a very special day in France, and some of my earliest memories are concerned with the national celebrations. Once, when I was seven and Hilaire five, we were taken for a picnic in the forest of St. Germain and then proceeded to the splendid Terrace where we stood all the evening looking at what Bessie described in a letter as "the most magnificent and poetical spectacle ever seen." A huge semi-circle of light shone from one end of the horizon to the other: all Paris was illuminated, and what was enchanting were the red lights on Mont Valérien which recalled to my mother Vesuvius in eruption. Fireworks were being let off in every village in the wide valley of the Seine, and from a boat on the river which flowed just below the terrace. Many of the houses were illuminated, and the trees were hung with lamps, even where there were few to see the magic spectacle.

On the *Quatorze Juillet* of another year, Nurse Mew was luckily having her summer holiday in England, so, when my grandmother was safely reading in her room, and Hilaire was resting with his mother, I persuaded our French maid Ada to take me to Bougival—a mile or so away—where I knew there were to be gay goings-on. Bougival was the quiet riverside town where our butcher and fishmonger lived and whither I walked on Sunday afternoons—always accompanied of course—to pick up any letters from England at the post office, as otherwise Bessie would have had to wait for them until Monday. So cunning a child was I, and so afraid that owing to the heat, my mother would not allow this expedition were she to hear of it, that I persuaded Ada to avoid the high road in front of the house and take the pretty shady lane which, if longer, was a pleasanter way of reaching the steep, rough hill which branched off the main road and led straight into the heart of Bougival.

When we left this *raidillon* I was delighted to see the gaily-dressed crowds in the town, composed for the most part of students and their girl-friends from the Latin Quarter of Paris. A group of them were gazing at a white poodle which was at once the pet and advertisement of the local cleaners-and-dyers, for he was shaved in the fashion of the day but his tufts of hair were dyed in various brilliant colours, thus advertising his master's skill. Ada was taken aback at the large crowds and the unusual appearance of the town *en fête,* but I coaxed her to go on to the wide paved roadway which bordered the river. There the scene was truly enchanting, for the Seine was covered with little boats each containing a man and a girl, the girls charmingly, sometimes fantastically, dressed in muslin frocks and large straw flower-bedecked headgear, while their cavaliers wore velveteen jackets and large picturesque black or brown felt hats.

On our way home a little horse-drawn carriage passed us. The driver looked back and called out to Ada asking if we would like to take a little drive, and with relief and pleasure —for it was very hot—we got into the carriage. He turned his old horse and began driving along the river-side towards the *Machine de Marly,* and I implored Ada to allow me to pay a visit to this famous water engine. I had only seen it once in my life and remembered it with a strange mixture of fascinated fear and passionate interest. The *Machine de Marly* was indeed a remarkable and fearsome sight, with its great iron wheels whirring round and round in the Seine providing water for the beautiful central basin on the Grande Place of Marly-le-Roi.

Afterwards I must have been looking very tired for Ada generously decided to pay the man to take us back to La Celle in his carriage. So off we drove, going very slowly up the steep high street through the gaily-dressed crowds of young people. I gazed with amazement at the students who looked so unlike the conventional young men who came to our house. As the carriage passed by the property of some old friends of my grandmother I felt alarmed, afraid that some member of that austere family would see me and report what they had seen. The carriage drew up about a hundred yards below the gate of our house and we crept quietly in, after Ada had paid the man two francs fifty centimes which was the modest fare in those days from Bougival to La Celle. When I walked through into the cool *grand salon* I realized, with a feeling of guilt and relief, that my absence had not been noticed by our mother or our grandmother, for they were both reading upstairs, and Hilaire was still with my mother.

I very well remember Hilaire's sixth birthday on July 27th, 1876. The day began with a funeral, that of a very old woman who up to the day before her death had been weeding in the vast kitchen garden of the Château which was overlooked by all the windows on one side of our house. She began her work at six in the morning, and she was paid five *sous* an hour. She was happy and cheerful, and kept herself clean and tidy. A few days before her death she had met Bessie, smiled and laughed, and said pretty things about Hilaire and myself, expressing the hope that Madame Louis would go on coming to France and not retire to live in her own cold and distant country. Bessie felt sad at her death, for when she and Barbara Bodichon had made that memorable stay at the Châlet when she first met my father, she used to wake early, and she always saw the old woman hard at work.

At her funeral I held the hand of Mademoiselle de Montgolfier, while Hilaire accompanied my grandmother. After lunch, we went on a wonderful expedition to a lake, which was still the private property of Napoleon the Third. It was a beautiful piece of water covered in places with waterlilies. We delighted in going there, the more so since there was a little deserted summer-house where we were able to take our tea. On this occasion we asked my mother, as we sometimes did, to tell us a story, and it was my turn to chose the subject. It was to be something we had never heard of before about Henry VIII and his wives. But she had already told us all she knew, and so Hilaire said, eagerly: "Tell us something about your youngness," and, as I begged for something exciting in order to amuse him and satisfy my own love of drama, she told us about two girls who had been at school with her at Leam, one of whom had stabbed the other. Someone had plugged the cut artery with a ball of lint and this had saved the girl's life while a doctor was being fetched from Warwick.

The birthday ended, to the disapproval of Nurse Mew, by Hilaire and me sitting up to late dinner at which all our favourite dishes were served. These included a *coeur à la crême*—that is, a heart-shaped cheese made of slightly sour cream and served with masses of powdered sugar.

It was on this birthday that Bessie wrote to a friend: "Hilary asked me today how I knew him to have been a little boy and not a little girl, and he asked 'Is my mouth larger, and my teeth more carnivorous?' When I told him the reason, he thought nothing of it. The body means so little to him; human relations interest him and trouble him. He asked what relation he would be to Nurse's children, if she had any, and when I found it impossible to answer straight away, he suggested after some thought, 'Perhaps Grandfather?' "

It was fortunate that we spent so much of our childhood in France, for the French are a clever people and are not astonished or particularly interested in a clever child. Hilaire's kind of cleverness did not arouse great interest among our relations.

In the France of our day there were many eccentrics. But none of them seemed to me strange. I used to wonder secretly why they were laughed at, and, as I had a feeling heart, it used to make me indignant to see people of all types go off into fits of laughter as they watched a certain Madame Bernard, an elderly village lady go off to pay a call seated in a wheelbarrow, which was pushed along by her gardener. I can see her now, a stout, comfortable looking woman, dressed in a black bombazine dress, a voluminous cape, and a big bonnet tucked up in a huge *brouette,* which must surely have been made to order.

Our childhood was steeped in history. We knew the Palace of Versailles from infancy, for our grandmother was acquainted with the curator and we used to be shown the apartments not open to the public. Even then I disliked the huge paintings in the public rooms commissioned and, I believe, actually paid for by the square metre by Louis Philippe. They were supposed to immortalize the glories of France. The Proclamation of the German Empire in the great Hall of Mirrors was horribly vivid to me all through my childhood and made me shrink from going through it. Bessie taught us a great deal concerning the old régime and as soon as I was able to read French she put into my hands what, to me, are the most remarkable memoirs ever written, those of the Duc de St. Simon. So Versailles was peopled for us by the men and women who made history there.

Bessie also used to take us to the Palace of Saint Cloud. Some of the rooms were of peculiar interest to her for it was there that Charles II's sister, Madame Henriette, had lived much of her short life in exile, first as a little girl and then, later, after her marriage to the brother of Louis XIV, and it was here that her strange and tragic death took place. Not unnaturally, she was said to haunt this Palace. The first to see her spirit was the Duc de Vendôme who was sleeping in a room which had been her boudoir, near one of the great reception-rooms. The Duke was still dressed, standing by the bed, when a door opened, and he saw the princess, whom he had known well, coming slowly towards him. He gave a cry of horror and she disappeared. Dumas *père* describes, in his novel *La Princesse de Monaco,* the Duke of Monmouth and

Madame de Monaco walking to a small lake in the hopes of seeing her ghost. Suddenly in the moonlight they saw the shadowy form of a woman. She waved her hand, and Monmouth rushed forward calling: *"Ma tante, ma tante Henriette!"*

Our life in London, where we spent each winter, was perhaps happier for Bessie than our life in France, for it was less filled with memories of her husband. She never went willingly into the garden at La Celle after Louis' death, though she would take us for walks in the beautiful countryside.

We lived in the little house in Great College Street of which the lease had been left to Bessie by her uncle Josiah on his death in 1871, though once we spent the winter with our grandmother Parkes in Wimpole Street. Though typically English, Bessie had unconsciously adopted certain French ways. For instance she seldom went out to pay a call on a friend without being accompanied either by Hilaire or myself. This astonished and rather shocked some members of her English circle, for in those days and for the following fifty years, English children of the type born in Bessie's London world were rarely seen by their parents' friends, and lived an entirely nursery existence.

In London Bessie picked up the threads of her English life. She again became intimate with George Eliot. "There is everything in Marian's books except genius," she wrote to Barbara Bodichon, "wisdom, wit, tenderness, an amazing knowledge of human nature, high principle of a very deep kind. . . . I consider that her books are conglomerate rocks, not granite or crystal. There is more of the living burning fire of genius in one page of *Wuthering Heights* than in the whole of *Romola* or *Daniel Deronda*."

She also wrote to Barbara Bodichon that she "was pleased

to renew old acquaintance. . . . The children and I have just come from the Phipson Beales, who live in Phillimore Gardens, and there I saw Alfred Watts and had a long talk with Mr. Caldecott. The room was full of old friends. Ralph Caldecott is absolutely bloodless in appearance. Not a trace of wit in his face. It is a mere mask to so much that is behind. We saw Jenny Lind yesterday. A quaint old woman; I could hardly make Mary realize that I had seen her in *La Fille du Regiment."*

Every Sunday Bessie and I used to go to see Mrs. Proctor whose daughter Adelaide, the poet, had been my mother's closest friend. Mrs. Proctor was a very old lady even then. She disliked children but made an exception in my favour because I was my mother's child. I was extremely quiet, and used to sit on a small chair, silent and observant. All the great literary figures of the day met in this drawing-room. Young as I was, I was struck by the vitality of Robert Browning, for whom my mother had a great regard.

Bessie had known Mr. Browning for many years, and at one time in her youth he had been an enthusiastic admirer of her verse. On one occasion she asked Mr. Browning if she might bring me to tea. We went to a house which I dimly remember, and he received us in a pleasant room. He spoke with affection and great admiration of the work of his only child Pen, who was then becoming known as a painter.

Later, soon after the publication of Froude's *Memoirs of Carlyle,* Robert Browning wrote the following letter to Bessie: ". . . I do indeed regret deeply the conception, execution and publication of those memoirs, equally unwise in their praise and unworthy in their blame; but I knew the extraordinary limitations of my dear old friend—and of his 'woman' too—just as well forty years ago as today. His opinions about men and things one inch out of his own little circle never moved me with the force of a feather—or I should hardly have lived five minutes of my whole life as I have done and, for the remainder of it, please God, shall do. But we must not ourselves prove ingrates for a deal of love, or at least benevolence, in deed and wish. I must not, anyhow. So, instead of 'burning Carlyle and scattering his ashes to the winds,' I am on a committee for erecting a monument to 'True Thomas'—whose arm was laid on my shoulder a very few weeks ago.

"He confessed once to me that, on the first occasion of my visiting him, he was anything but favourably impressed by my 'smart green coat'—I being in riding costume; and if then and there had begun and ended our acquaintanceship, very likely I might have figured in some corner of a page as a poor scribbling-man with proclivities for the turf and scamphood. What then? He wrote *Sartor*—and such letters to me in those old days! No, I am his devotedly and—if you permit me—yours cordially, Robert Browning."

Bessie was devoted to Lady Augusta Stanley and to Dean Stanley. One day he met her in Dean's Yard and said with a twinkle in his eye: "I dreamt that I had been elected Pope, and I said to myself with despair 'It will be in the *Times* and all over Europe tomorrow; what will my friends think?' And this question put me into such agony that I awoke!" It was at the Deanery that Bessie had first met Mrs. Rundle Charles in 1870. They became instant friends and formed a friendship which meant much to Bessie's ardent nature and temperament.

Mrs. Rundle Charles wrote *The Chronicles of the Schonberg-Cotta Family* which became a best-seller in England, and later went all over the world. In some ways Mrs. Charles was more remarkable than her work. She was a highly intelligent and cultivated woman and to some she possessed great charm;

she was the only daughter of a well-known member of Parliament, and was already a widow. She was an enthusiastic supporter of the Church of England and many of Bessie's letters about religion were written to this friend. I never found myself in sympathy with Mrs. Charles, but she became and remained a good friend to Hilaire till the day of her death. It is for this reason that I bring her into my story.

Bessie always took the liveliest interest in politics and she remained a Liberal, though in November, 1876, she wrote to a friend: "I have seen so much to blame in both phases of political thought that I am disillusioned. Indeed the one creature I really care about, and who I long to see more happily circumstanced, is the agricultural labourer."

Bessie had always been a poet and a visionary, a being who lived in another dimension to that where dwelt ordinary men and women. And yet unlike most visionaries she had immense sympathy with men and women in any kind of trouble or anxiety.

Utterly different as were my mother and I, we were in close sympathy with regard to what were then called "the Rights of Women." Somewhat to her surprise, I announced when I was eight years old that I intended to be a woman doctor. I had become fond of Dr. Elizabeth Blackwell, that remarkable American lady, who was a close friend to Bessie. I asked if I might be taken to see Mrs. Garrett Anderson. My mother was amused when after my wish had been granted, I remarked, "Now that I have seen this other doctor, I feel Dr. Elizabeth is made of marble, and Mrs. Garrett Anderson of asphalt."

Lively contact with the French family was maintained during the periods in London. A letter from Bessie to my aunt Louise written from Wimpole Street in 1876 thanks her for her Christmas presents, and gives the following item of news: "The children are invited to a School Feast on Friday, where they will see our English Cardinal. Hilary heard him preach on Christmas Day and whispered to me: 'Is *it* a Woman or a Man?' " She goes on: "I see with real regret in today's *Times* the death of M. Mohl. I fear it will make a sad blank in the life of the old lady whom I always love for much past kindness, and to whom I was so singularly indebted in regard to my marriage. [It was she who had sent Bessie and Barbara Bodichon to La Celle for the first time.] There never was a more striking instance of *l'homme propose, et Dieu dispose.*"

Bessie was still profoundly unhappy. *"Ma vie est finie,"* she wrote to my aunt Lily several years after she had become a widow. She also expressed a wish to die, saying that her son and daughter had been born too late, and she hoped time would reserve for them happier, more complete lives than had been their mother's. She became terribly nervous whenever either of us was ill, even with the usual little illnesses of childhood. And yet she wrote: "It is a blessing that there is a constant necessity for attending to the children. They are both very well and I think, if I may say so, they are both very pretty."

She gave much anxious thought to our future. "I have been telling the children tonight that *serving* God means something active, not only what they call 'being good.' It is so difficult to help children to serve; and yet I believe it would remove half the difficulty of making them 'good.' Human creatures can't *poise*. Even the wild bird cannot do it for more than a moment; and the spiritual wings not even for that moment."

And again: "I am anxious to start my daughter early in life with the power of making a moral effort. If I could only find out the path Marie will naturally follow, I will do everything on earth to help her follow it from her earliest years. I feel so anxious about this child, for I am fully conscious that the particular Puritan training which I received and which embodies my idea of a good sound education would never really suit this ardent little creature. . . . She is full of energy, and has no taste at all for intellectual pursuits. In that she is the very reverse of Hilary." This was written when I was just seven years old.

Meanwhile Hilaire began to recite little verses of his own, and this is one Bessie wrote down:

> I had a little Fly
> I called it Silver Wing
> And over little bits of thread
> This little Fly would spring.
>
> I made it little hedges
> Of little bits of thread;
> And I made a stick-Memorial
> When this little Fly was dead!

He was also interested in anything to do with mechanics, and noticed everything that was worth noticing. I can recall Bessie's pleasure at the eager way in which he enjoyed a visit to the Soane Museum in Lincoln's Inn Fields. At six he was already reading both French and English.

Around this time our grandmother Parkes wrote the following description of us to our grandmother Belloc: "Dearest Madame Belloc. Our children are well, there is never anything the matter with them, and each is mentally satisfactory in his or her way, though dissimilar. Marie has much practical good sense, and great observation. Hilaire has more original, but not more valuable, qualities to my mind. He will become more *sage* and less self-willed as he grows older; rather imperious at present, and I think his grandmother Parkes is his *bête noire* as she insists on observances as to comparative trifles, but which all aid in forming manners. Their mother is devoted to them. She teaches them every morning. They really make good progress, and as they are almost constantly with her they gain much incidental knowledge in the course of the day. They ask endless questions and she is always patient with them in answering and explaining. She is more at rest teaching them than she would be were she not thus occupied."

My grandmother Parkes died suddenly in 1877, after which my mother spent an unhappy time in 17 Wimpole Street. She was lonely and uncertain what to do next, and had only recently consented to stop wearing mourning for her husband. There was a wedding in the French family, for which event her two sisters-in-law, Louise and Lily, gave her a dark green silk dress from Worth, covered with black lace.

I have retained loving memories of my grandmother Parkes. As seems to have been so often the case with women of her generation who "enjoyed ill-health," Mrs. Parkes appeared to grow stronger every year. She kept her delicate pink-and-white complexion, and when I knew her a lace cap, threaded with narrow ribbon, rested on her curled white hair. She had been much amused and pleased when an old gentleman who had known her in youth came up to the carriage in which she, Bessie and I were sitting, took off his hat, made a sweeping bow, and exclaimed: "Let me greet three pretty women!"

Bessie told me late in life that at this time my grandmother Belloc more than once pressed her to consider a second marriage. A Frenchman of our family circle approached my aunt Lily and asked whether her sister-in-law would consider an offer from him. She could also have married again in England. But though she approved of second marriages for others, the thought of following such a course herself never touched her mind.

3

THE BOY WHO SINGS ON
DUNCTON HILL

➛➤➤❮❮❮

Two years after Nurse Mew came to us, Hilaire had had a bad attack of what would now be called influenza, and Dr. Atkin, in whom Bessie had complete trust, said that in his view it was essential that Hilaire should spend most of the winter in the country. My mother and I went to Arundel in Sussex and called on a kindly old priest who advised us to go to Slindon, a village four miles from Arundel, to look for lodgings for Hilaire and Nurse.

Slindon was, and still is, one of the most beautiful and unspoiled villages in West Sussex. It lies high up in a fold of the Downs, six miles as the crow flies from the sea. Slindon had what to us was all important—a Catholic church. Slindon House had been one of the rest-houses of the Archbishops of Canterbury in the Middle Ages, and the sanctuary lamp in the private chapel had never been extinguished.

My brother's devoted love of Sussex dates from this stay, and it was during that first winter in Slindon that our nurse, Mrs. Mew, took down the following poem:

> While it was snowing
> And the wind was blowing

And the ship was going
>   The Frigate Eurydice;
While prayers were being offered from the deck,
On came that cruel cloud to wreck
>   The Frigate Eurydice!
>   Just passing round
>   By Ventnor Town
>   The ship went down,
>   The Frigate Eurydice!
Whilst royals and studdings were spread out wide,
The ship heeled over on her side,
>   The Frigate Eurydice!
Only two were brought ashore alive;
Now they are completely revived
And now they are going to dine
>   To the Frigate Eurydice.
Steam tugs were sent, and they did try to save,
But full three hundred found a watery grave
>   In the Frigate Eurydice.

Hilaire had been deeply impressed by the loss of the *Eurydice*, a man-of-war which had been caught in a great storm, and had gone down, almost every one on board being drowned.

Nurse sent the verses to Bessie, and told her how surprised she had been when my brother had insisted on her taking them down from his lips. He was then seven.

Hilaire was a reserved little boy, and had none of the high spirits and *joie de vivre* which I had always had. From then on he either dictated or, when he began to write, wrote verses, and now and again Bessie would send them to our French grandmother.

From early childhood, Hilaire took an intense interest in verse, and in what is called verse form. He soon acquired a remarkable knowledge of both English and French poetry. I think most of his reading was done in youth, for in later life unlike his mother and sister, he did not read much for pleasure. This in a sense was strange, for all his relations, both in France and England, were eager readers. In fact, it may be said that with almost every one of us, literature, both French and English, old and contemporary, was our principal intellectual interest. In those days Hilaire shared our deep interest in reading as a pastime. In a letter to me Bessie writes: "I am reading *Ivanhoe* to Hilary every night when I am at home and he likes it enormously. He says he had no idea Sir Walter Scott was like that."

A year later, when Hilaire was nearly eight, Bessie decided that the family should move to the country and she chose Slindon, as Hilaire already knew and loved it. She gave up Wimpole Street (left to her by her mother) entirely, but kept on the little eighteenth-century house in Great College Street, though she let it furnished from time to time.

Her reasons for the move are contained in a letter to grandmother Belloc written on July 12th, 1878, from Wimpole Street: "This is the last time that I shall date to you from the familiar old house. The quitting seems to throw different epochs of my life so very far back; my brother Priestley had been dead eight years when we came here, and that was just twenty years ago. . . . I sometimes feel as if I did not know how to bear the responsibility for the health, happiness and education of so many people; but I feel convinced that at Slindon all the unconscious forces of air and water and perfect tranquillity will work with me. There is a social current in England now which is not good; a relaxing of first principles in all directions, and I believe the best way to counteract it is to bring young children face to face with nature, with farm life, with animals. One must either do this or be incessantly watching what they see, hear, read and talk about."

Bessie took a lease on Slindon Cottage on the advice of an old friend, Lady Georgiana Fullerton, who had lived there herself for some time. The Slindon estate was owned by a Scotsman called Charles Stephen Leslie of whose numerous children six survived. When Bessie took Slindon Cottage, Mrs. Leslie was living a life of dignified retirement with her children in Slindon House. While the move was in progress, Bessie was staying with her friend Mrs. Charles, from whose house she wrote instructions to her very young son: "Darling old man, don't let any papers be put on the walls till I have chosen them! We must have the same colours as we had in Wimpole Street because of the pictures. I'll bring you an elephant of some sort. The grey cloth sort have gone out of fashion; species extinct!" And there follows the yet more cryptic: "I hear that Black Spanish fowls are the best to buy."

This is the first intimation of a strange experiment in an effort to make money that Bessie made at this time. With no experience whatever, except childhood memories of the chickens at Leam, she decided to keep poultry.

She gave grandmother Belloc an account of her activities: "I have quite decided to put all my farming energy into fowls. Any other animal we will only keep for household use and economy, but not with any idea of business. And this is what I have done: I have bought two families of the very best French race—the Houdans from Gambair-les-Houdan near St. Cyr. Major Nott, who breeds fancy and prize fowls for his amusement and to keep his six children in eggs, sold them to me. I have one cock and four hens, whom I call the Royal Family; and another cock, a tremendous fellow, and five hens, ever so much bigger, whom I call the Imperial Family. These creatures lay, but seldom or never sit on their eggs. Providence must have created them with special anticipation of Monsieur Rouillier-Amoult's *Incubeur!*

"I paid a very heavy price for the creatures—200 frcs. in all for the eleven, but I was very glad to find Houdans of the best breed in England. They live in separate places—the Royals in the large stable yard, and the Imperials in a kitchen garden which I have sacrificed to them. And I have watched them, and fed them, and made much of them; and on Monday, going to the Royal Pavilion myself, while my young gardener was driving Nurse to Arundel, what should I see but two eggs on the brick floor, one, alas, broken, but one beautiful and sound. . . . There will probably now be one or more each day; and I hope the Imperials will not be long before they begin. The eggs are going to be added to the Incubator tomorrow.

"As to eating them, one could not think of such a dreadful sacrilege. One might almost as well think of eating the Queen's grandchildren!"

The letter ends: "Now about the house. With all the pretty old furniture and the Italian pictures it looks a most beautiful abode. The dining-room, the middle room with a large window facing south, is a very warm room. The drawing-room at the western end is very long, but I have a comfortable corner by the fire. Dr. Priestley's portrait, the large one which you may not remember, is over the fireplace and the family miniatures of which I have half a dozen, all round it. I have papered this room, which is long, large and low, with oak paper, perfectly plain, and the pictures show up on it admirably. I have a long low bookcase about three feet high, and on it is Colonel Swanton's miniature, a set of curious old china and some alabasters brought by my father from Italy forty years ago. The dining-room is papered olive green and is as nearly as possible the exact reproduction of the room where we had the wedding breakfast. The third room, much smaller, has in it all the furniture from my dear mother's boudoir."

Needless to say Bessie soon discovered that, instead of making, the fowls were losing money, and before long the beautiful Houdans were being given away in pairs to any of the village people who would accept them. But her love of Slindon remained as strong as ever: "How I wish you could see this place, more beautiful even in the autumn than I ever saw it before, perched as it is on its high chalk hill, and in sight of the sea."

Slindon Cottage was not only a charming house but, what became increasingly important to my mother as time went on, it could be let for a considerable sum each year during Goodwood race week. Our life there was a simple one—for those days. That is to say we had three servants who had been for many years with grandmother Parkes: a gardener, a gardener's boy and a groom—for a friend had given Bessie a pony carriage.

And Hilaire wrote more poetry. The following was enclosed in a letter to me, written when he was nine: "Dear Mary, I hope that you are quite well. I send you my last poem, 'The Nameless Knight,' that figure in Mr. Izard's church that Mama called the nameless knight. I send you also a picture of a frigate. Nurse sends her love."

THE NAMELESS KNIGHT

There is no name upon his grave
If his grave it haps to be
And his face doth look towards the plain
And towards the calm blue sea.

He lies in a quiet church aisle
With the small churchyard in view
By a little Gothic window
And 'neath a shadowy yew.

He may have been carved for ages
And oft heard the tolling bell
And he may lie for ages more there
In that church aisle—who can tell?

There is no name upon his grave
If his grave it haps to be
And his face doth look towards the plain
And towards the calm blue sea.

He had already discovered the strength of repetition.

During the first Christmas holidays at Slindon Bessie wrote in her diary: "I walked with Marie up to the Folly, a curious sham ruin on the top of the highest hill in the neighbourhood. The view from there is wonderfully beautiful; a vast landscape seen through rolling mists. We sat on an old harrow and I taught the child the points of the compass which, strange to say, she does not really know. She has an extraordinary difficulty in technical acquirement and yet is so queerly wise."

It was about a place near Slindon that Hilaire wrote the following poem which he copied out in a clear, bold, round hand, and illustrated with little drawings:

On yon hill stands an old grey tower,
Age after age, and hour after hour.
On one side a moat, so large and deep
On the other a precipice so steep,
On the third a ruin, perhaps the bower
Of the Baron who lived in that old grey tower.

The old grey tower it looks on the hill,
Through the twilight and midnight still,
Like the ghost of the castle of ancient days,
With their queer old sayings and curious ways,

Like a shadow when night begins to lower,
Is the outline dim of that old grey tower

The tower by moonlight—pale and still,
When the clacking is heard of an ancient mill,
When its shadow is cast down the moonlit hill,
Where there lies at the bottom a sparkling rill,
But a cloud o'er the moon at the darkest hour
Hides at length from our sight the old grey tower.
                    J. H. Belloc. *Fête St. Louis MDCCCLXXX*

Hilaire's and my education was naturally a constant pre-occupation with Bessie and she feared we would lose our knowledge of the French language. Soon after the move to Slindon she wrote to grandmother Belloc at La Cille Saint-Cloud, the following letter: "I have made up my mind to engage as tutor for the children Monsieur Leheribel who taught the son and daughter of Marie's godmother. He is old, but still vigorous, and a very good teacher. He will give them regular lessons each day, and I shall feel his being at Slindon a comfort, for I have known him slightly for many years and it gives me pleasure to remember that he knew Louis. I know that both the children ought to begin their real education. True, our little Marie reads without stopping—history and biography books by the dozen and the hundred; she knows Jane Austen's novels almost by heart. Yesterday she was reading Arthur Helps' *Friends in Council,* today she has attacked the first volume of the early years of the Prince Consort. But, as more than one of my friends has pointed out to me, she is quite ignorant of geography and grammar.

"As for Hilaire, he is in high delight at a visit to an exhibition of electricity. He was particularly interested in an incandescent light which can burn four months at the bottom of the sea. The exhibition gives me a queer eerie feeling of treading on the very threshold of the unseen universe. Voices from a distance—lights springing into brilliance out of darkness—vibrations thrilling through the air. . . . I had hoped country life would open the children out, but it seems to be driving them in on themselves. Marie cares for nothing but reading. As for Hilaire, he seizes the clue of metaphysical science or scientific metaphysics in a way that I do not care to encourage."

My brother's extremely active mind was shown by a curious little plan, or pedigree, he made at this time, in which he marries invention to progress. Their offspring are steam, telegraph, telephone, phonophone, and air pumps, etc. Progress descends from Wise Men, through Law and Agreement, while Invention has Necessity (knows no law) for a parent.

Monsieur Leheribel arrived in the spring. He was nearer seventy than sixty, and belonged to a type of Frenchman unknown in England. He was priggish, obstinate, conceited and high-minded. He brought with him to Slindon Cottage two huge cases of books, and hoped—it was obvious to me, young as I was, though not to my mother—to settle down with us for life.

I still vividly remember his arrival at Slindon Cottage. My mother gave him one of our most pleasant bedrooms, and he also had the use of a sitting-room. He was a tall thin man, and always wore a black frock-coat; also, which fascinated Hilaire and myself, a bright brown wig.

As I loved everything French, I was prepared to become attached to him, but soon I grew to dislike and fear him. He was extremely conscientious, and gave up many hours of each day trying to teach Hilaire and me French grammar. The only bright spot was the fact that the children of Mr. Izard, the Rector, joined the class. But M. Leheribel was an indifferent teacher, or perhaps had become so from age. Even my brother, who enjoyed learning, made no headway with him. As for me, I learnt nothing, and after a while my mother wrote to a friend that her little Marie did not improve with Monsieur Leheribel in any way.

She discovered with surprise that during the forty years he had lived in England, he had only once gone back to France, neither had he made any effort to keep up with French thought. He even refused to glance at the French newspapers, which were sent by my French grandmother. By the end of that spring he presented a serious problem, for my mother had now come to realize with dismay that the old man fully believed he had settled down for good.

Patient, understanding, and astonishingly long suffering, in my view, was Madame Swanton Belloc in her relationship with her beloved English daughter-in-law. One of my mother's peculiarities was that of often changing her plans, having meanwhile completely forgotten any circumstances that would make this change inconvenient, and sometimes impossible to carry out.

Thus, on the 30th of June 1879, came a letter from Madame Swanton Belloc reminding her that by her wish, our house at La Celle Saint Cloud had been let for a couple of months, and that therefore it would be impossible for us to go there for the summer: "You told me, my darling, that you did not intend to come to France till the autumn, and that you thought it would be a good thing for the house to be inhabited. Lily found the only kind of tenants any of us would care to have, people we know, and who will be careful of everything. So, if you come before say September 1st you will find me in Paris."

Madame Swanton Belloc had given up going to the house she loved and where she had been each summer for a number of years, to please her daughter-in-law. In the same letter she spoke with some anxiety of the education of my brother: "I feel unhappy concerning Hilaire. You tell me that you are thinking of making him into an engineer as was your uncle, Mr. Parkes. But has he any vocation of the kind? If so, he does not get it from anyone in his father's family. You tell me that Marie is growing up into 'a wild country girl.' This makes me uneasy. Surely the time has come when she ought to begin to be taught habits of self-government and of the kind of order which should play a part in the life of every woman. I am certain by what you say that M. Leheribel is a disappointment, and that you would find a good governess in every way preferable. There is an alternative for Marie. Why should she not go to a convent for a year, or even two years? But find an Order where the nuns are intelligent, well-educated women and lacking completely what we call *bigoterie*. Can you persuade her to write to me once a week, just a few lines written by herself and without having first made a rough copy? Her last letter was obviously written from her heart and gave me great pleasure."

And then came a few words concerning the Prince Imperial: "You say nothing of the death of that unhappy young Prince. I never believed good would come from that expedition. I should like any details you may learn. It is a terrible loss for the party, which I hear is breaking up in spite of everything said to the contrary.

"Adieu, my darling. This letter may prove to you that I still am well enough to love you with all my heart, that I am filled with a longing to see you. I do not ask for much, simply that you should write to me every fortnight a few lines. Tell me how you are in yourself and how everything is going on. God be with you, my darling and beloved daughter."

Not long before we were leaving Slindon, and starting for

our autumn visit to La Celle Saint Cloud, Monsieur Leheribel suddenly expressed a wish to accompany us. My mother, little knowing the good fortune about to befall her, wrote to Madame Belloc: "I fear you will not like having Monsieur Leheribel, but I feel sure I can find him rooms in the village. In any case, I could arrange for him to have his meals at the Châlet. Please tell me frankly how you feel about this? If you don't like the idea of his coming to La Celle Saint Cloud, I will tell him he will have to remain at Slindon, or visit some of his friends in England, till our return."

My grandmother, however, was curious to see this fellow-countryman, whom she knew was not only becoming a problem to her daughter-in-law, but also not turning out to be a satisfactory tutor. So Monsieur Leheribel accompanied us to our French home. After a short time Madame Belloc found we were making no headway, and also that my mother dreaded spending the following winter in his company. So she undertook to give him his *congé*. Madame Swanton Belloc did not reveal what my mother only found out after her death, that when she told him he was not to return to Slindon, she gave him three thousand francs, which was, I suppose, a year's salary.

Poor Monsieur Leheribel! He is the only Frenchman I have known well in my long life whom I have heartily disliked. He undoubtedly believed what was, however, untrue, that I deliberately set myself to avoid benefiting by his tuition.

So that autumn, it was decided that I should be sent to a convent school. And Bessie made up her mind to let Slindon Cottage furnished, and to live for a while in lodging at Hampstead, near to her friend, Mrs. Rundle Charles. There, for a time Hilaire attended Heath Brow School in preparation for the Oratory School at Edgbaston.

The Heath Brow School report for the term ending Easter,

1880, says that Hilaire was top in Latin but adds he was "clever but rather idle." In French he was second out of two. He took an interest in geography, made rapid progress in chemistry, and was top in arithmetic. He did "fairly well" at drawing and his conduct was "good." He must have been well-grounded at Heath Brow School, for when Bessie decided to send him to the Oratory School, though he was only ten years old, he was put into a class with boys two or even three years older than himself.

From Hampstead Bessie wrote to grandmother Belloc: ". . . meanwhile Hilaire and I are very happy living here in Hampstead. I was telling him today about Byron, pointing out that from our windows we can see Harrow where Byron was at school. I did not tell him of Byron's poor little daughter being buried there, just outside the graveyard walls. Today is Hilaire's half-holiday and he is going to the Zoo with Nurse. He is getting on very well, full of spirits and interested in everything."

In the course of 1880 Bessie was told, to her astonished distress, that she must leave Slindon Cottage, as the eldest son of the owner of the Slindon Estate had married and wished to live there. She was in two minds as to what to do. Should she take another house at Slindon, or should she go back to La Celle? She wrote to Barbara Bodichon: "My dear, there is always La Celle Saint Cloud; after all, it is my own and my children's true home, and I am always well in health when there. But it would be terribly lonely for me when Madame Belloc was not there; also, how would my children be educated? I feel I can come to no decision."

The place Hilaire and I loved best in England when we were children, was Madame Bodichon's Sussex home. It is called Scalands—it had been called Scaland's Gate—and in our childhood it was a real cottage. We were welcome at all times, and especially after we had had some childish ailment. Being with us there was a great pleasure to my mother. She had always loved Scalands since early youth. Again and again she mentions taking her children for walks in the beautiful Sussex country, feeling how strangely the old scenes and thoughts blended the past and the present. Our happiest days were when "Aunt Barbara," as we had been taught to call her, was there with us. Hilaire was convinced there was a wolf in the wood, and he was very anxious to see it.

Our mother wrote: "We live in an enchanted palace in a wood. Food and wine noiselessly placed on tables; flowers without and within; hundreds of books, French and English, old and new. Marble busts; Nollekins of Charles Fox; two cats, snowy white owls; and the old clock which once chimed at Clapham to Wilberforce, chimes on." She adds: "Have you seen in the French papers that George Eliot has re-married? It has made a great noise, as she is close upon sixty and her husband, Mr. Cross, much younger. He is described as a very good fellow, about forty-two, and intensely devoted to her. I have seen a letter which she wrote from Italy to Barbara—we neither of us knew anything about it till the deed was done."

Barbara Bodichon was Bessie's most intimate friend and my mother could write to her about the subjects nearest to her heart. ". . . The whole question hinges on the problem of the supernatural. If people think there is no supernatural world, they had much better say so. I think there is, and that its existence is attested by a great variety of evidence. But it does not at all shock me when people say that they neither perceive nor believe it. I expect a gradual scientific revelation; an unfolding of the laws of the Unseen Universe. Professor Huxley in his discourse on my great-grandfather Priestley hinted at this. One thing is clear scientifically: Matter has only a phenomenal existence. It is protean and the mysteries of force are so great that we are now only on the edge of them. Little questions about the creed of the Church of England are almost too small to be picked up on the point of the controversial scissors. The Church of Rome, being much older and wiser, tries in her best minds to squeeze out the inner meaning of the facts. . . ."

So it was natural she should consult Barbara when she found herself suddenly without a home. And naturally the education of her children was of paramount importance in the decision she made. They had become almost too much for her: "The children are both of them so much cleverer than I am that I get confounded! I suppose the old grandfather Belloc, whom I never saw, was a real genius."

On the other hand the pull towards France was very real as can be seen by letters from La Celle: "As I was walking along by myself on Tuesday evening it was deep twilight and the last faint glimmer of sunset was dying over the thickly wooded hill. The great round moon rose from the skyline and I thought with great thankfulness of the years spent in this lovely place; of the dear dear husband whom I had followed to his resting place up that wooded hill; of the terrible sense of despair which with time has faded, of my children who I feel love me so deeply. I stayed out nearly an hour, and when I went back I was afraid I should find the whole house in alarm at my absence, but the old people were in their own rooms and so it had been unnoticed."

And about her and Louis' Paris flat, to a friend, shortly coming to France: "You will be in our *faubourg*, my *faubourg* where I lived such a happy tender domestic life. I can still see my little Marie toddling about in the Luxembourg Garden. We lived in a few large rooms, looking across a beautiful garden on to Saint Sulpice. For a long time after Louis was taken from me I could not endure to see even an engraving of that side of Paris."

Then again Bessie must have been swayed in her decision by financial considerations. On the death of her uncle Josiah Parkes in 1871, she had inherited a considerable sum of money which, carefully invested, brought in about £1200 a year—ample for the Louis Bellocs' way of life. But after the death of her husband and her mother, Bessie was induced by the son of an old friend to allow him to embark on a series of gambles on the Stock Exchange. The result was that at the end of two years all she had left was the small income produced by the Parkes Trust Fund, a trust of which she could not touch the capital.

She gradually became more and more involved in money difficulties through the recklessness of this man, though much time went by before the dangerous position into which she had drifted became apparent to her. It was a serious misfortune that she had no men friends whom she trusted, to whom she could go for advice, though she had a certain number of distant English relations, one of whom was her trustee. But they had disapproved of her becoming a Catholic and of her marriage to a Frenchman. I was about twelve years old when I first realized Bessie's anxiety about money, for there came a day when she was made aware that a large part of her capital was gone. The young man in question wrote her a note of agonized apology and then left the country.

What Bessie finally did in 1880 was to move to a smaller house in Slindon, and no sooner had she taken the lease of Newlands, as it was called, than she wrote to grandmother Belloc saying: "I have a great longing for some permanent habitation, and I have been wondering whether after all it would not have been best for us to settle down at La Celle

Saint Cloud. If I took my mother's furniture over to France our beloved house would look again what it looked like before the war."

I described Newlands as follows to grandmother Belloc: "It is an old house which belonged to a family called Newland for three hundred years. It has a pretty, old-fashioned garden, stables, outhouses and a field. Opposite to Newlands is the Rectory which is very nice. The rent is forty pounds a year, a third of what Slindon Cottage used to cost Mama."

Newlands lacked the amenities which had made Slindon Cottage not only delightful to us all, but also easy to let. Indeed I cannot remember Newlands being let at all. Though far smaller than Slindon Cottage, it was more difficult to run. There was a dark sitting-room on the ground floor, the one drawing-room being on the first floor. Close to the front door was the village pond. Our fine old furniture looked out of place in what had been a farmhouse—indeed the pleasantest room in Newlands was the kitchen. The walled garden had charm, and there was a small meadow.

However it was while living at Newlands that Bessie wrote her collection of essays which was called *In a Walled Garden*. The first edition of the book has on the cover, inset in gold, a sketch made by Hilaire of the back of the house. This part of Newlands was much older than the front and very picturesque. Twenty years later in my second novel, *Barbara Rebell*, I laid the scene at Slindon and described Slindon House, Slindon Cottage and Newlands, but all the characters in my novel were imaginary.

It was strange that Bessie did not set herself seriously to make money by writing. She had published several books, all of which had been well reviewed. When now and again she wrote an article—always on a literary subject—in one of the

Marie and Hilaire

Bessie Rayner Parkes,
their Mother

Hilaire, aged 12,
at La Celle Saint Cloud

A Letter from the Oratory School

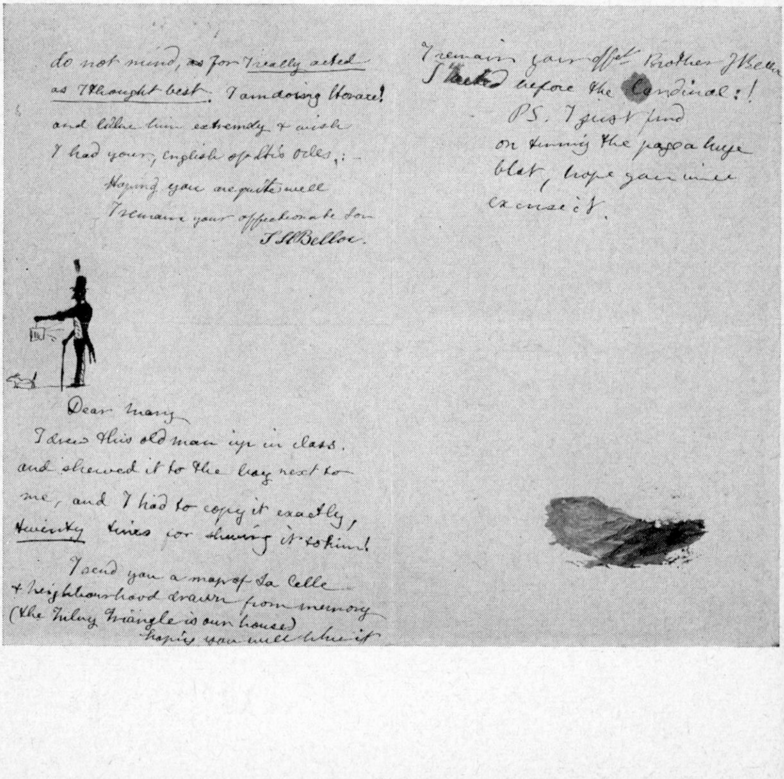

[handwritten letter, partially legible]

do not mind, as for I really acted
as I thought best. I am doing Horace!
and like him extremely, & wish
I had your English of this Odes; —
Hoping you are quite well
I remain your affectionate Son
J. H. Belloc.

Dear Marie,
I drew this old man up in class,
and shewed it to the boy next to
me, and I had to copy it exactly,
twenty lines for shewing it to him!
I send you a map of La Celle
& neighbourhood drawn from memory
(the Ruby Triangle is our house)
hoping you will like it

I remain your affct. Brother J. Belloc
I kneel before the Cardinal; !
P.S. I just find
on turning the page a huge
blot, hope you will
excuse it.

monthly reviews, or in a weekly such as the *Spectator*, her work at once attracted interest and attention. But she was extremely modest about her writing. I have only a very few letters that mention it at all.

"You ask when *La Belle France* was written; at divers times and seasons over an interval of years; but the paper on Sens was begun *there*, the first two pages written on the spot and finished, I think, after my marriage. The book was printed in the first year of my married life and the preface written then, as well as the verses about Sens. I came *from* Sens to La Celle Saint Cloud. . . ."

It was at this time when Bessie was so unsettled that she wrote the following very true picture of Nurse Mew to grandmother Belloc: "Sarah Mew's beloved Bible says 'Take ye no thought for the morrow' and 'Blessed are the poor in spirit' —but her lifelong habits assert that as it is winter eggs had better cost threepence apiece and children should each have twelve hats and fourteen frocks! Add to this republican principles (which I detest) and a desire to keep the Sabbath on hymns and the history of some Jewish King addicted to strong language, and you have the whole woman, dear Maman."

The unhappy year of 1880 ends with a letter to Barbara Bodichon written on December 31st. "This is the last night, almost the last hour of the year and my thoughts go out to you as they did last year from Paris. It has been a sad and tragic year for me. Mary Merryweather and Mademoiselle de Montgolfier gone—two such landmarks in my life. Also, although I saw but little of Marian Lewes of late years, I thought of her often; I do not know that I considered her as much as you did an integral part of our generation." [Bessie took Hilaire with her on, I believe, the last occasion she ever saw George Eliot. It was a regret to me I had not gone too.] Then comes a moving addition to her letter: "It is now four o'clock in the morning, New Year's Day, the hour when the Sisters of Charity get up all over the world. I often think of them when I wake about this time. When I first became a widow I used to tell myself that if my children married early I might join the Sisters of Charity if, that is, they would be willing to take me. I did not think I should be too old at sixty. I had decided to give all my possessions to my children."

The year 1881 contained a great sorrow, too, for my grandmother Belloc died. Bessie had felt that the happiness of the family reunions at La Celle could not go on for ever. "I felt when I was at La Celle as if everything was almost *too* bright to last. All the children and grandchildren and great grandchildren healthy and prosperous, my Louis the only absent one, and Madame Belloc, the old lady of 84, as keenly alive to every phase of politics and literature as she was twenty years ago." My mother and I went to Paris at once when we heard my grandmother was critically ill and we had the comfort of seeing her before she died.

Bessie's great breadth of sympathy and of feeling was shown to a striking degree when she became virtually owner of our two houses at La Celle. She shrank from letting the Châlet, where she had lived such happy years with Louis, but she often lent it to people who she thought required a holiday. Going one day to Paris to see the nuns of the Congregation of the Holy Child, she suddenly made up her mind that certain of the Sisters ought to have a change and rest. So she wrote to the Mother Superior and suggested that the nuns at Neuilly should come out to La Celle and stay in the Châlet. Only Catholics of an older generation will realize how surprising was the suggestion. However, permission was given and I have before me a letter from the Mother Superior:

"I do not know how to thank you for all your kindness to

me and my Community. The thorough change which we have
all had at La Celle Saint Cloud has been greater than we can
describe, and the pretty Châlet, and the walks in the beautiful
woods will long be remembered by us all. It was such a pleasure, dear Madame Belloc, to get to know you and your two
children, Marie and Hilaire. It was so fortunate for us that
you were at La Celle Saint Cloud at the same time as we were
there. The lovely place, with its dear mistress and sweet children, will often be the subject of our conversation and, oftener still, remembered in our prayers."

Some time later Bessie came in contact with the head of the
Salvation Army in Paris. She found that the *Maréchale,* as
that lady called herself, was married to a man who had been
a distinguished official in India. They had a small baby who
was suffering from the heat. At once my mother insisted on
the mother and baby coming to the Châlet, only making the
stipulation that the Salvation Army should not attempt to
proselytize any of the people in the village. I remember the
excitement and astonishment their presence caused in the
neighbourhood, for to French eyes the Salvation Army uniform was both extreme and unbecoming. We saw a good deal
of these ladies, and when we came back to England Bessie
met, and much respected, the famous Mrs. Booth.

Hilaire and I were both much distressed by the death of our
French grandmother who was an integral part of our lives.
We now had no grandparents left. We had never known our
two grandfathers, but Bessie was adept at keeping the person-
alities of our forbears constantly before our minds. The following extract from a letter is an example: "Do get the memoirs of Madame de Remusat, which give such a picture of the
'interior' of General and Madame Bonaparte as one never
thought to see published. Fancy Grandmère being one of a
cortège of young ladies who went to meet the Archduchess

Marie Louise with flowers, when she passed through Rocroi, of which Colonel Swanton was Commandant."

But it was perhaps for Bessie's father, Joseph Parkes, that Hilaire had the greatest admiration. I remember him finding a secondhand copy of his grandfather's book, *A History of the Court of Chancery,* and how delighted he was, for copies were rare.

Joseph Parkes was a remarkable character. In my opinion had he devoted himself entirely to any one of his many interests, he would have left a mark on his generation. He had a passion for politics, and though successful in his own legal profession, he made public affairs the main business of his life. It is acknowledged by those interested in the Reform Bill agitation how great and how active was the part played by Joseph Parkes. It was to him that Lord John Russell wrote a letter in which occurred the famous phrase: "It is impossible that the whisper of a faction should prevail against the voice of a nation."

His great generosity was perhaps one of the reasons why he habitually spent more than he earned, although he had a prosperous career as a Parliamentary solicitor. His brother Josiah, at that time at the height of his successful career in civil engineering, again and again came to his aid. Finally Joseph was offered, and accepted, the post of Taxing Master in Chancery. This provided him with the fixed income of two thousand a year.

The great literary interest of Joseph's life, and it is curious that it should have been so, was the Junius controversy. He was convinced that Sir Philip Francis was the author of the then famous *Letters of Junius,* and he left a mass of material concerned with the life of that strange and mysterious human being. He was preparing a book on the subject when he died suddenly in 1865. Bessie, after her marriage, wrote to her mother: "In the *Revue de Deux Mondes* of September 15th is an article by M. Rennaut on Junius with a very nice mention of my father. I shall send it to you."

I give Joseph Parkes' epitaph which was composed by a group of his friends: "He was earnest, truthful and wise. So he won the confidence of powerful men, and his name will stand on the list of British worthies who promoted the measure for the reform of Parliament, the reform of the municipalities of England, the reform of charitable foundations and the reform of the Court of Chancery. These were his chief public services. How kindly and generous he was in private life, how dear to many friends, how deep the sorrow at his death, can be only known to those who caused this stone to be erected as a lasting memorial of their own grief and his great work."

I have discovered in Hilaire's and my ancestry on both our French and English sides such strange, original and noble-hearted people that I believe they are responsible for much that is mysterious in Hilaire's character, and they account too for the diversity of his gifts.

4

THE ORATORY SCHOOL

->>><<<-

WHEN Bessie made up her mind to send Hilaire to the Oratory School which was then at Edgbaston near Birmingham, she wrote from Paris the following letter to Cardinal Newman:

"September 6th, 1880. Your Eminence, I desire to place my little son under your care at the approaching term. His name is Joseph Hilaire Belloc and he is just ten years old. He is great grandson, on the maternal side, of Doctor Joseph Priestley, and he has a pronounced taste for all natural science. His religious instruction has been commenced by Father Arden of the Dominican Priory, Haverstock Hill. He is a good little boy and has never hitherto been separated from me. I write from Paris, but my home is at Slindon near Arundel."

As a result of this letter the Cardinal invited her to come and see him. I, of course, accompanied Bessie on this visit, and the Cardinal made an immense impression on me. He wore a red biretta, red stockings and a vivid broad red band round his waist. His pectoral cross was attached to a gold chain. His voice was very weak.

It interested us to learn that he was never addressed by the

Oratorians as "Eminence" but as "Father," while he addressed his priests by their Christian names. We learned he was extremely independent in his ways. He got up at five every morning, made his own bed and dusted his own room. After which he said Mass in a part of his sitting-room which had been partitioned off and turned into a little chapel. He had an enormous correspondence, and this was greatly increased on his birthday, also on the feast of St. Philip Neri and on the feast of St. George from whose ancient church in Rome he took his title.

That September, Bessie wrote from Edgbaston: "Nurse and I brought Hilary here and have launched the dear thing at the Oratory School, among sixty boys, managed by thirteen Oratorian Fathers with old Cardinal Newman at their head. The teaching masters are laymen. Hilary is very delighted to go."

Before leaving Edgbaston, Bessie heard a sermon preached by Cardinal Newman. "Was I not fortunate to hear one of Dr. Newman's sermons, and on such a subject too? He defined the Catholic position with respect to the Scriptures very clearly, explaining why they had sometimes been burnt, and with a certain quiet breadth of assured conviction which was imposing in its simplicity. It was like four square walls of plain, polished granite. Commanding greatness, compared to which his accidental position or popularity in the English branch of the Church is a matter of utter indifference, was the effect on my mind. York, Canterbury, Westminster seemed all three completely dwarfed. He suggested a rational Augustine (if you can imagine such a thing) . He is not nervous, like Dr. Manning or Dean Stanley; he looks very *old* but not delicate, and when he speaks the look of age disappears; nor is the face sad like the portraits. There was the ghost of a smile on his face as he wound up with the words: 'There are a great many excellent books for spiritual reading, but I think the Scriptures are the best.' "

Bessie chose the Oratory School for her son because of her great regard for Cardinal Newman. But, characteristically, she made no enquiries as to the way the school was conducted. From her letters it is plain that she believed the Cardinal took an active part. This was no longer the case, even if it had ever been so, for he was then an old man and though he preached, I believe, every Sunday to the boys and occasionally saw one of them for a short time, he had nothing to do with the management of the school.

Here is another testimony to Bessie's admiration: "I think spiritual success an occult thing, and that if by 'teaching boys at Birmingham' Dr. Newman made *one* saint, that saint might outweigh in real good all the sermons he might have preached at St. Mary's, Oxford, as the modern Bossuet. It is desperately tempting in moments of illness and weakness to read beautiful lives of beautiful circles of people who were like our garden roses for fullness of bloom and perfection of culture; but the entire resignation of that old man's life, his steadfast grasp of that which he believes true, his silent repudiation of that which he believes untrue, his contented certainty of pleasing neither party and his utter indifference to any sort of world, seem to me the greatest example of our generation.

"Putting aside the question of dogma altogether, and supposing with the great majority of England that his dogma is all a mistake, still is it not wonderful to see the *man*—the man who *The Times* calls the modern Bossuet, and of whom Nurse's dissenting paper says that 'in John Henry Newman all the Churches of Christendom can feel that they have a part?' I believe this extraordinary authority which honours his name is due not so much to his power of intellect, because great as that confessedly is, most English people think he has used it untruly or too subtly, but to the veneration felt for a man who, having all things within his grasp, has shown himself successively indifferent to any form of human respect. It is of the very essence of my conception of Christian faith and practice that people bear witness for Christ by what they *are*. That a dumb saint in a garret might conceivably convert a nation. Only get the centre incandescent and it radiates, and we know no limit to the radiation."

In addition to her reverence for Cardinal Newman, there was a further fact which played its part in Bessie's choice of school for Hilaire. She was proud of her grand-grandfather Joseph Priestley's connection with Birmingham. We passed his statue close to the station every time we went to Birmingham to visit Hilaire. In Bessie's opinion one of the most interesting days of her life was the one when she was present with her mother at the unveiling of that statue. Huxley made a long speech during which, as Bessie expressed it, "he touched upon, but with a shrinking finger and with what I felt to be a faint longing after, Dr. Priestley's firm faith in God and immortality."

Hilaire's first letter from the Oratory to me at my convent at Mayfield gave his time-table: "Dear Mary, we have rather long hours, up at 6.30, Mass till 7.30, school till 9, breakfast till 9.30, lessons till 11, working till 12, play till 12.10, work till 1, dinner till 1.30, play till 2.30, work till 5, play till 5.30, work till 9." And to Bessie: "Dear Mama, I felt very homesick at first. I have had another tooth stopped and it hurt very much indeed. The decay went right up into my jaw. I found *Paradise Lost* the other day in the library. I can climb a smooth pole 18 feet high. I ran 2¼ miles also and did not feel any the worse for it; on the contrary rather the better. Give best love to Nurse and thank her for the 'Boys' Own

Paper.' Your loving H. Belloc." He usually signed himself H. Belloc both to Bessie and myself, even at the age of ten.

Luckily he enjoyed games thoroughly: "Dearest Mama, I have been learning to skate, I can't go very fast but I am learning. Please send me some wooden skates, and please try and send them in a box because paper slips and breaks. The snow here is quite as high as at Slindon. Happily Father John made a decree that we only get up at 7." And at the beginning of the summer term, when he was still only ten: "I don't feel a bit homesick. We have begun cricket which is awful fun. I liked your letter, please send a long one on Monday. . . . I tell you what I should like. I don't think I really can stay here after my twelfth birthday, but I will be all right till then. Please write to Father John about my learning to draw."

And he loved his work. "I am working on as usual and half laughing at the kind of fun it is to work and how delicious it is to go to bed after hard work and play, it is really glorious to have summer, for it is always raining here during the winter and smoke curls about in the midst of it, ugh! . . . We have been doing the story of Ximenes in Greek and it is very nice. The drawing master is taking an interest, and showing me how to work. Please ask Mary to send me some holy pictures."

And the following, when he was eleven: "If you like I will bring my Ovid home in the holidays and read you some of the beautiful things in it. I think that as regards school it is hard, but then nothing is made easy and because the battle is close up, so much the more reason for fighting it. . . . How nice it must be for you to be at Dublin, is it a dirty or clean town? I never can think of Dublin without imagining it to be *very* dirty. I don't know because I've not read much about it, but I have no doubt you like it very much. I am sorry I cannot write more but I wrote in an examination today which took me three hours! And rather a stiff one so I am rather knocked up. You asked me to send you some illustrations, so I send them."

While he was at the Oratory School Hilaire constantly illustrated his letters to Bessie. Slight as they are, these pen and ink drawings are remarkably good. In one of his letters is a spirited drawing of a horse and soldier. He wrote: "I have been making attempts to draw horses—the first horse I have ever tried to draw. They are supposed to be four horses yoked to a chariot and suddenly checked."

The "typical school-boy" is apparent in some of his letters: "Monday was the Cardinal's birthday so we had veal and Yorkshire pudding. Actually it seems in poetic language 'a vision of the past and a golden dream of heavenly future.' Please send some jam with the cakes and *soon*. . . ." "Please send one of those pound boxes of Cadbury's chocolates."

Very early in his school career he made friends with James Hope who remained his friend all his life. "Yesterday I stood on one side of a stream and my chum James Hope on the other; I was in Warwick and he was in Stafford; we played cricket in Staffordshire but we bought refreshments in Warwick. As a train was coming on, I cried out 'Fellow over the rails' and after that my chum said 'Poor fellow, how mangled he is,' which literally frightened a workman near us and made him look over the rails with us."

But some astoundingly mature reflections on friendship for a child of eleven were inspired by a boy called Lennox of whom there is no mention thereafter. "When I read *Enid* in Tennyson's *Idylls of the King* I feel very happy, but very odd. . . . I was so very fond of Lennox when he was here, and I don't think he saw it, though he was very good to me. We always were so much more together than I am with anyone else just now. I wonder what is generally thought of friendship?

I think it is the brightest angel Earth has, perhaps Heaven also."

The discipline at the Oratory during these years seems to have been of a very mild nature. There is no mention in the large numbers of letters which I possess of any corporal punishment. Milder forms of punishment are sometimes referred to: "Dear Mary, I drew this old man [sketch] in class and showed it to the boy next to me, and I had to copy it exactly *twenty* times for showing it to him." "Dear Mary, we beat Oscott for the first time for ten years in a cricket match. The Oscottians were wild thereat—observe [sketch]. This is the captain in agony [sketch]. Here is our best man—he made the most runs ever made at the Oratory [sketch]. As I write a wretched infant is kneeling out *en pénitence* [sketch] while the awful master eyes him [sketch]. I ought to be working now but the master sees me not and all innocent of my misdeeds chides me not. Oh my studious comrades! This particular boy is known as 'fatty,' is impudent and good natured [sketch]."

For the Easter holidays of 1881 Bessie decided, with little preparation, to take Hilaire travelling in Wales. He remembered this tour all his life. He wrote: "I understand by your card that I am to go to Wales, and that you are coming for me. *Please come early*. This term has been much nicer for me than last term. I am getting liked and I am getting stronger. My legs are getting frightfully strong."

From Wales he wrote me one of his most vivid letters: "Dear Mary. We went up Snowdon yesterday. I had a frisky pony that danced and capered in a very nasty place betwixt two precipices, and the worst of it was that I was the 'front of the caravan,' Mama's pony being a fat, cumbersome, comfortable, brown, easy-going, steady and altogether nice pony led by the guide, called (the pony I mean) Jenny; my brute was

Willie (which by the bye rhymes with hilly, I mean to make a poem on it) .

"Up at the top, bread, cheese and beer was served out. It was at 27 Fahrenheit or a sharp frost, snowing and violent wind, ground as hard as a pancake, only seven yards across, with three little cottages; beer nearly frozen and one gentleman proposed drinking it and then sitting on the hob till it boiled, but we took the wiser method of not sitting but setting the bottle on the hob, till it nearly busted.

"When at a nervous part, the guide gave us a most delightful account of the men who had got killed on Snowdon. We went down the other side down a precipice of more than 45 degrees, or halfway between standing upright and embracing mother earth. The rhyme 'If I had an animal and he would not proceed' may be verified here as the wolloping would ensure a pleasant ride through space, of which the terminus might prove very uncomfortable, alias going down a precipice. When we were at the bottom we rode part of the way here (Capel Curig). The quiet Janet being in front, Willie began to try to get in front of Jenny. Now there was not room for this, but gallant Welsh Willie took about six steps backwards, then a run and a trot, onwards, faster, and came into Jenny with a tremendous concussion and nearly broke my kneecaps. Jenny, the gallant mare, stood the charge most wonderfully.

"There was an embankment across the lake just wide enough for one horse, and two of course if in single file. Now here Willie put on a gentle trot but jolting so that every moment I feared that he and I might have a good insight of 'newts and toads and slimy things that in the water swim.' Yours affectionately, J. H. Belloc."

Bessie and Hilaire reached Carnarvon on April 19th. She

wrote: ". . . I went close to Pen-y-law. I looked at valley and mountains with a moved heart. The place seemed bigger and wider than formerly. My own outlook is so much wider than it was at twenty-four. Some day perhaps we shall look at our little planet from the wider horizon of the spheres. . . . My eager little boy draws with a passion of love. Sometimes I think he will be an artist and not a civil engineer. He is a little flame, pouring out poems, parodies, calculations, metaphysics, till I am frightened to hear him. He knows more Welsh in a week than I have ever known."

Few letters seem to have survived from Father John Norris, the Oratory headmaster (to whom Hilaire refers in his letters as "John"), but the following news is luckily among them—written in May, 1882: "Hilary will make his First Communion on Corpus Christi; he is preparing himself for it very nicely and thoughtfully, and Fr. Pope, who is instructing him, is very much pleased with him." And from Hilaire after the event: "My first Communion has made a great difference to me, there is always something by me in the Blessed Sacrament, something to place entire confidence in, which is the really great want I have felt here."

His religion meant a great deal to him. In a letter to me he says: "The Retreat begins on next Wednesday: I like it but a great many boys don't. I keep a little book of all that is said and enlarge on it on my own account." And: "The last sermon we had was a very wonderful one on the Resurrection, and it was an unusual subject; that when the three Maries came to the sepulchre they wanted someone to roll away the stone and they found that two angels had rolled it away for them. I thought it was such a beautiful subject. . . ."

And a letter to Bessie when he was not yet thirteen: "These kind of days which are cold and dull with a good wind

driving the clouds about are so nice here because it gets dark
early, but not too early and the chapel is all a beautiful grey,
you can only just see the colour on the pictures and it makes
them so beautiful, and the sanctuary lamp looks so bright and
yet lights up so small a space, one can pray beautifully as the
day is beautiful. I think that beauty and love, and things
which people generally look down upon as not stoic or heroic,
are the essence of heroism and manly feeling, and this because
they are the essence of God as we hear of Him and understand
Him. I felt this in chapel today, that the light feeling which
proceeds from love of something and of something beautiful,
is not a feeling that will pass, but the happiness of angels in
the love of God. Have you ever felt that in one of those beautiful churches, Notre Dame or St. Ouen, how one loves the
beauty around one so much that one is convinced that it was
the grace of God, as well as man, that helped to build that
church?" And he enclosed a poem:

> To some thou art a memory of the past,
> Notre Dame
> Of a faith that long has fled.
> And to some thou art a poem wrought in stone
> And to some the tinted light thy old panes cast
> Breathes a spirit lost and dead,
> This alone.
> But on thy front I see the master hand
> Of my race
> And turret, oriel old and gargoyle, all
> Are a glory they alone of men could trace.
> Frank is Frank and Gaul is Gaul,
> And to me thou art my people and my land,
> Notre Dame.

Hilaire wrote to me very often, and I preserved all his letters. In one of the longest he wrote: ". . . I am now reading

Oliver Twist with great interest. I know the story of *A Tale of Two Cities,* but it is too much drawn to the life which I am so well acquainted with, to read at school. I might read it at home, but it would upset me here, I think. I remember how wonderfully he described the six carts going just the same route as Marie Antoinette went; and I was so struck with his mentioning that the false Evremonde was innocent —the word has a double meaning in the sight of God and even in the sight of the most brutal executioners of the Revolution.

"I am getting a friendship with Homer. When I shall be able to draw well enough, I shall draw and paint them as I imagine them and it will be a great pleasure to me. When one sees such a wonderful landscape as from Snowdon, it is the counterpart of Troy, Snowdon is the height and shape of Ida and half nestling at the foot, and the mountain road where we saw that wonderful effect of sunlight on Caernarvon. If that wonderful place was inhabited and fought for by such men as Trojans and Greeks, then there would be nothing on which Dickens could write his worst scenes of bloodshed and sneaking. Then if a man stole, he stole openly, and if he stole meanly, he was considered a coward. Now the art of theft is to do it as much in the dark as possible! There would be no 'dregs of the People,' no 'lights o' London.' Then rich or poor, or rather great or small, stole alike; now it is the peculiar appendage of the weak, because they cannot so much as live without it!"

There is scarcely a letter written in 1882 and 1883 (when he was twelve or thirteen) which does not contain some allusion to the art and literature of Greece and Rome. "I am getting fonder and fonder of those 'mighty minds of old' who put forth the affections and beauty of life so wonderfully. There are some passages in the *Iliad* which make me thrill with pleasure; there is a corresponding sound within me, like the waves, sounds strike their own chords in the ear. And my chief pleasure is that they are so real—the old Heroes, and want of any kind is always filled up by the sympathizing character of Homer; he told the truth and made no man a saint."

And: ". . . Corinth of two seas, too grand to witness and yet not to please. Do you like the picture? It represents Corinth, the water near you is the Aegean Sea, while that opposite is the Gulf of Lepanto."—This was accompanied by one of his very best sketches.

And: "I send you a lot of sketches taken as a rule to illustrate some of those really splendid pieces in the *Iliad*. I have begun the *Odyssey* and it is just the same as ever, only more beautiful. After the ridiculous theories which everyone preaches now, that no such thing as love exists without selfishness, it is quite refreshing. People of course who say that friends are the supernumeraries of life cannot be expected to judge why the Greeks were noble because their whole system was founded on the love of *something;* to Socrates it was the Unknown God, and in Homer's time I think it was the love of that power they did not understand which enabled them to love the beautiful around them.

"I send you a poem . . . the idea being the whiff of cold Atlantic on Grecian Ulysses, one of the most lovely things I ever read is the description of himself which Ulysses gives to Alcinous, it is so beautifully *naif*. He says: 'I am Odysseus, being of little Ithaca, a farm land; now my fame is great and reaches into Heaven.'

> But most when evening comes I seem to hear
> The sheep bells tinkling on the heather-height,
> And the loud whirring of the birds' low flight,
> Hieing them westwards as the darkness falls.

And comes to me the sight of all most dear,
The woody dell which nestles round the halls
Which are my end; aye, and that only face
Which I have waited long and may not see.
Memories so sweet they flood a barren place.
Where mine eyes, weary of a restless sea
Grey-hearing, yet as having lost its scope
Of changing mood comes dark upon my hope,
And chills my soul with sad monotony.
Through the black waters as of old to roam
Were freedom; rather look I on the blue
And pierce its narrow boundary till all fair
Against the rosened East I seem to see
Beyond my prison bars of circling foam
That which my hard fate will not give to me.
Rest, and the heath and all surcease of care,
Strong in the waters, Ithaca my home!

"We are doing in class the Apology of Socrates; get a translation; it is his speech before his death and is marvellous. He spoke it 400 years B.C. It is what you call Christian."

Again: ". . . The weather is fearful here and getting up at half past six is beastly because so dark. I do not mind getting up at five for that matter, but I do wish the sun was shining.

"I have begun Cicero. He is just like a man speaking in Parliament, only rather more excitable. I wish you could find that translation of Horace, I want it so much. Has there been a frost in France yet? We are to go in for the Oxford Local Public Examination at the end of the year. I do not know whether the examiners will come to us or we will go to the examiners. I hope I take a place because it will show me my real position among a lot of boys. . . . Do you think my writing is at all better?"

At this time Bessie was distressed that Hilaire's handwriting was not at all clear or good. It remained childish till he was about fourteen, then it turned suddenly into the small clear script which he kept to the end of his life.

Bessie's impression was that the Oratory was in every way the opposite of a Jesuit school. If a boy cared for learning, he was able to learn, but if he disliked school work, as do most boys, little effort was made to teach him. Hilaire always took a very high place in the subjects he cared for. Scattered throughout his letters are reports on his progress. At an early stage: "I have good news to tell you. I was top in last term's exams and have got a head-remove with the two chaps below me; it is the class I have wished to be in so much; in it you first begin the Latin poets, Euclid, algebra, all the things which I like so much. I used to be so desolate here, without a friend; but a new master came the other day and he understands me, he opened the way and though the battle is there, it is possible to fight it and a great weight is off my heart. Why I hated everything was because no-one had broken the ice for me, now it is all right. I am in a truer, happier state of things than I ever was before."

And, later: "I have some chance for the prize the Duke of Norfolk gives. . . . We do our exams *on paper* with a vengeance, our Classical Prize alone took six days at the average of five hours a day. It was great fun; I got another boy to wake me at half past four and prepared till half past six in the morning. It is delightful to wake in the early morning."

Bessie wrote in her diary an account of Prize Day for that year, 1884: "Hilary has gained a most extraordinary series of prizes and I believe the scale of study under Cardinal Newman is high. He has got the Second Norfolk Prize [a classical prize—£5]—never yet won by a boy under fourteen—also the first English Prize against the two upper forms united. He won it by an essay. Also the Fourth Form Prize. He was also among the first competitors for three other prizes and won a high number of marks for each. It was pleasant to see the old Cardinal stand up and present them. Very imposing did the old man look with his white hair falling on his scarlet cape. As to my laddie, he took his successes very modestly. There followed a banquet after the prize-giving. The Cardinal was not at table, but he went through the rest of the day gallantly, including the Latin play."

Hilaire's comments on the school are interesting: "I think the tone of the school is getting better and healthier; there is more honesty and boyishness, and the narrow spirit has less influence. I say less, which is not saying much."

Hilaire was always given important parts in the annual Latin play. He was an excellent actor, using his hands while he acted—his French blood, I suppose, made this second nature. From early childhood he had a remarkable memory. He wrote: "They have gone through the play once already. I have been told by the critics all my faults, but those that do not try to find fault, or that do not profess to be judges—and this represents the audience for the most part—seemed pleased with me."

And a long report on the Oratory School play in a local newspaper for July 1884 says: "It is very pleasant to be able to speak in such hearty praise as we can of the performance last night [the play on this occasion was the *Aulularia* of Plautus]. From the rise to the fall of the curtain the play (and it is a difficult play to act) went without a hitch, and the young actors and their tutors are alike to be congratulated on a very remarkable success. Where all were so good it seems invidious to particularize . . . . and in the two female characters of Eunomia and Staphyla, Kennedy and Belloc were splendidly 'made up' and evinced genuine talent. . . . Cardinal Newman, who has always taken the greatest interest in the getting up of these plays, was present to witness the triumph of the Oratory pupils."

In a letter to me, whether or not referring to the same play I do not know, Hilaire says: "I am in the play as an old woman who snaps and snarls, but my voice is too high and I squeak instead."

Scattered throughout Hilaire's letters are references to the people he loved: "Nurse asked about my health. I feel better than ever and am quite well." "Could you send me a few *pots* of honey—it was kind of Nurse to send it in the comb but it gets squashed and was messy last time." He adds "What was Grandmamma Belloc's finest work? Did she ever translate Byron?"

It would be impossible to exaggerate how much Hilaire's French heredity meant to him. It was a happy day for him when he was given the watch which had been worn by his great-uncle, Armand Swanton, one of Napoleon's officers, at the Battle of Waterloo. The watch had saved its owner's life by deflecting a bullet.

He was very contemptuous of school French: "I am getting on pretty well in my French this term but I hate learning French rules, they do *me* no good of course because all the French I know is innate, I don't think of the why and the wherefore of my manner of putting a sentence."

The following discovery obviously fascinated him: "I discovered to my great astonishment that I was of a brachycephalic race anterior to the advent of the Gauls and thoroughly Latinized ! ! ! That is, I was wondering the other day whether or no I was truly from the South and now truth reigns supreme, for lo! 'The people of this (Provence) quarter of France are distinguished from the Franks of the North by their round heads, faces circular rather than oval and short stature!' Fits me to a T! Therefore you are now with those who are my true compatriots; and you must be enchanted to hear that that lovely country is covered by a people who are as brachy-cephalic as the Archaic Plaesoicforms or Pteroldyctls in the Miscene period."

This was written to Bessie while she was staying in Cannes in the south of France. At this time Bessie writes: "Hilaire has sent me such a pretty poem for my birthday. He is a good young child!" At the top he put the date—June 16th, 1885.

> Where the blue sea rolls on its foamy tide
> Washing the shores of my lovely land,
> Breaking against the rocks in stubborn pride,
> Scatt'ring the myriad diamonds on the sand:
> Where heaven to earth her loveliest hues has lent
> To deck herself with more resplendent grace
> And to crown all, her noblest ornament
> The dark-eyed children of my native race—
> There art thou now. And from this frozen north
> My little birthday message I send forth
> To reach thee in thy bright bejewelled clime
> Hoping that these few lines which I have sent
> May breathe the spirit of my good intent.

This feeling for France made him want to spend our holidays at La Celle. Where to spend the holidays must sometimes have been a problem, and Bessie wanted her children's views. "Dearest Mamma, I noticed a clause in your last letter to the effect that you were in doubt as to whether we should go to France or not; and I write this to tell you that *if it is indifferent* to you, and you will not mind going, I for my part am longing for it. I am much fonder of La Celle Saint Cloud than I am of Slindon, for in the stress of life what I care for is my old home. It is our natural place, don't you think? . . . I should be glad to see the nuns again, and there is a great deal to do there."

In spite of these assurances, Hilaire must sometimes have been lonely at La Celle, for he goes on to ask Bessie if he can invite a schoolfriend to stay—"the ennui that I feel in the holidays is simply because I have no companion." He recommends his friend, Wall, to Bessie as follows: "I have a chum here whose father is out in India *à l'ordinaire,* but his old guardian has met, I understand, with some mishap in money matters, but be that as it may. I want him to come to La Celle some holiday or other. You have often told me nothing would be easier. He is one of those good-natured Irish boys with a strong brogue and national to his backbone, a thoroughly nice boy. He thoroughly revels in all those things La Celle can give—bicycling, bathing. It would be so nice for me to have a companion. He would travel at his own expense and, like all the boys whose parents are in India, he would have a sum put into his hands by [Father] John for the holidays. He usually spends his holidays with his brothers (who are younger) in the house of a relation in Galway, and it is rather dull for him. He would be no expense beyond food and washing, and he and I would enjoy ourselves so much. You need not fear any kind of foppishness—he has always travelled third, and the house in Galway seems to be not much larger than ours from description."

Hilaire mentions bicycling and bathing. I well remember how much he enjoyed long rides on his bicycle, and Bessie allowed him great freedom. He had only one bad accident, near Mont Valérien, when he was nearly fourteen. He fell off his bicycle at the bottom of the hill and was carried unconscious into a peasant's house. We did not hear for some hours what had happened. The man and his wife treated him with the greatest kindness, and sent us a message as soon as they learned where we lived. The bathing took place on the Seine, at a place which had the absurd name of *Le Petit Trouville*. It included a swimming-bath which had been cut out on the bank of one of the islands, and on hot days people would drive long distances to bathe there.

During my youth it was much cheaper to go from La Celle into Paris by a slow train than by what was absurdly called the *rapide*. Bessie was regarded by our neighbours and our French relations as being eccentric because we always travelled by the cheapest route and—what was to them more astonishing—second class. The difference in money, if the journey was short, was small. I remember thinking it strange that she should cause us to travel like that. I can remember no occasion on which Hilaire accompanied Bessie and me to Paris—he had his own special way of going. He walked to Bougival, took a tramway following the course of the Seine for an hour, and finished up in a train from Ruelle. Hilaire never cared for speed and I think he would have enjoyed going to Paris by river, but unfortunately the Seine steamboats which were a feature of our very young childhood had been replaced by the railway.

I think our happiest holiday was when we went all the way from England to Paris by boat. We crossed the channel to Le Havre and there boarded a cargo-boat going to Paris along the Seine. There was little traffic on the river except for a certain number of barges, and there were immense stretches of water with hardly any navigation. Hilaire's love of sailing and his love of the sea was the natural outcome of the life we led as children. I shall always be grateful for having gone to Paris in that way. What remains most vividly in my mind is the splendid sight of Château Gaillard, not very far from Rouen.

Another great attraction at La Celle Saint Cloud was the family Dutreux. We were as fond of the children—Lily, Emma and Auguste—as if they had been our own sisters and brother. Their grandparents owned the Château, the beautiful house which had been inhabited for a short time by Madame de Pompadour. As it was within five minutes' walk of our home we spent many happy hours there every day. Now and again our young friends came to see us, but not often, as their mother had a morbid fear of their meeting someone who might be sickening for an infectious disease. At the Château many remarkable people came and went, for the Dutreux and their cousins, the Pescatore family, had relations and friends in Belgium, Holland and Germany.

If Hilaire loved his French home, he loved it no more than I did.

When Hilaire and I had returned to school in England, Bessie wrote to us both very often: "M. Dutreux asked after you after Mass." Nevertheless she was obviously lonely and I am surprised she left me at Mayfield as long as she did. She did in fact take me away before I had finished my course, and I was sent to Queen's College, near Cavendish Square, as a day girl (we were back in Great College Street for a while). So Hilaire had me to consult if he were worried in any way about our beloved mother, knowing that I was with her. "She has not written for a week. Is she ill? If so, please do not mention it to her. But if she is not ill, she may have forgotten to write to me, so please remind her. . . ."

Her not writing would have been a very exceptional occurrence as she watched Hilaire's activities closely—not only his academic progress of which she was justly proud: "Hilary has got the Mathematical prize: £7 of books. It is a great honour, for last year he took the highest classical prize possible to his place in the school," she wrote to Barbara Bodichon when Hilaire was fourteen—but also his material needs. ". . . About your chair, you do not seem to have taken any from College Street. What do you sit in? I have a feeling that you are not comfortable and it distresses me." This was when he was old enough to have a study of his own at school. And she goes on: "I think of you so much, my Hilary; only think how close is the tie of mother and son." And on another occasion: "My darling, I am troubled about your money; did you ask Father John for what you wanted, or shall I send you a cheque? Don't get into any complication for want of telling me what you require."

This would seem to suggest that Hilaire suspected that Bessie had money difficulties, and yet this cannot have been so for he often spoke with regret in later life that Bessie never told him of her anxieties. He was certainly unaware that while he was at the Oratory his school bills were being paid by Elizabeth Phipson, a wealthy relative of Bessie's who lived in Edgbaston in a house called Westbourne where we sometimes stayed. It was a small manor house with a stream running through the garden.

It is curious that a boy who as a young man was to take a passionate interest in politics scarcely ever mentioned a public event in any of the letters he wrote from school. In fact there is only one allusion which runs: "The news from Khartoum is daily discussed here with great avidity. It is very sad news. If only we knew if Gordon were alive." The young writer seemed surprised that his mother did not visit the War Office every day to read the telegrams which at that time were on view for the public to read.

His interests seem to have remained chiefly literary to the end of his school days—he left at the end of the summer term of 1887, that is to say when he was nearly seventeen. By then he had been a prefect for a year. He wrote to Bessie: "Dearest Mamma, I have been made a prefect, with Hope. I am very glad. I was afraid that John was never going to make me one, but now there is a clear year." He had passed his matriculation, he had made various decisions about the future, he had had both a poem and a story published in national magazines, and he had fallen in love.

The first intimation that Hilaire had written a story comes in a letter to Bessie: "About my future, I thought I would tell you that if other sources fail, I have had a hint that the Duke of Norfolk could help me. . . . You told me these holidays that if I wrote a story you would get it in *somewhere* for me. Now I have written one. If you think you can raise the wind for me by getting it accepted please ask me to send it. You see, I should like some money to fit my study, in time I will write for some things from home; but I don't want to ask you for money."

The story is a remarkable performance for a boy of sixteen, but it cannot have helped with Hilaire's immediate financial needs for it was not published until May, 1888. It was finally placed in *Merry England,* the magazine edited by Wilfrid and Alice Meynell, and in the same number there is Francis Thompson's beautiful *Dream Tryst*. Hilaire's story, *Buzenval,* covers twenty pages of *Merry England* and tells of an incident in the Franco-Prussian War which took place near the villages Hilaire knew so well—La Celle and Bougival are mentioned by name. It shows deep love and knowledge of the French and deep knowledge of soldiering and the campaigns of 1870–1871 down to the smallest *sortie*. I give a short quotation:

Now it is a well-known fact that Frenchmen cannot fight well unless they have an opportunity to display *élan,* fiery charges and the rest; to all this there were on the day of Buzenval natural obstacles which could not be overcome. Imprimis the human body needs food, and the French army had eaten up the horses so that there were no cavalry regiments; secondly, the attack had to be made up hill in a fog; thirdly, the ground over which it lay was field-land, peasants' land, some of it ploughed, some of it planted with a thick growth of short brush, some of it full of grass running rank and high, all of it sodden and wet and muddy. Therefore it was no time for a charge. And yet the attack was to be made—how would they do it, these *Franzosen?*

Hilaire himself has corrected the copy of *Buzenval* that I possess and at the end he has scratched out "Hilary" as the Christian name of the author and substituted "Hilaire."

Unfortunately I do not know where Hilaire's first published poem appeared, and his letter to Bessie throws no light on the matter. In April, 1886 (when he was still sixteen), he wrote: "Dearest Mamma, I am so glad that Findlay accepted the poem. I was very proud, of course he took the 'ceaseless surging' . . . Swinburne has written a poem of the most admirable diction in the *Daily Telegraph* of today." Here is the poem, transcribed from my copy in Hilaire's own handwriting.

STORM

Fades the day glare into night,
Driving through the sadden'd sky,
Loud, tumultuous, rising high,
Sweeping towards the Western Light,
Comes the wind the wild waves urging;
Waves white-crested, rolling, rolling,
Darkly in the darkness gloaming,
On the strong sea's ceaseless surging.
And the cloud crest, half-seen form
Of the pale moon, upward toiling,
Looks affrighted on the boiling

Breaking waters of the storm.
Through the rent wrack casts around
Here and there a sudden brightness
On the foam top's silver whiteness
Silvering on the blue profound.
Down the land-steeps shrieks it seething,
Foam crests myriad broken sending
To the wind its wild way wending,
Murmuring like some creature's breathing.
As the stronger Soul, O Sea,
Light forwaken, terror haunted,
Struggles ever all undaunted,
Battling vainly to be free;
Strongly on thy strength relying,
On the unyielding earth thou breakest
And the cliffs stone heart thou shakest
In thine anger bond-defying,
Break the hiss in deepening roar,
On the stubborn rocks that bind thee
Raging, restless, ever more.

All through his school career, Hilaire's tie with James Hope
was very close and every year he spent part of his summer holidays at Heron's Ghyll, where the Dowager Duchess of Norfolk then lived. James Hope's mother had died when he was
born, and he and his three sisters were brought up by their
grandmother, the old Duchess. James Hope was in later years
Deputy Speaker of the House of Commons. Hilaire naturally
became friends with his sisters and his first love was the eldest
of the three girls, Minna, a pretty and unusual girl who later
became the wife of the distinguished ambassador, Sir Nicho-
las O'Connor.

Hilaire wrote to her from the Oratory: "Dear Minna, I
write to you at a time when there is not much news about. I

got a whack on the head with a cricket ball which has laid me
up; the doctor will not allow me anything in which 'my brain
may be excited!' I have been forbidden books, prizes and
exams, and the natural consequence is that I am slowly becoming mad, like the prisoner of the Bastille who was shut up
in the dark. It was too bad to let me work for the Religious
Instruction prize and then to prevent my going in for it."
After he had recovered he wrote: "I have been given a glorious part in the play, something really worth learning and
going in for. . . . My 'poetical compositions' increase rap-
idly."

Perhaps it was Minna who inspired the following verses:

> Eyes so bright ye may grow dim,
> Who knows?
> Love may die at Fancy's whim,
> Who knows?
>
> Summer water, Paradise,
> Where the swallow lightly flies,
> Winter waters, dark and chill,
> Will the bright bird haunt thee still?
> Who knows?
>
> Mounts the sun for ever bright,
> Who knows?
> Though that Love should live for aye,
> Though that Love should never die,
> Who knows?
> Who knows?
>
> Life may find a thousand fears,
> Which may drag through bitter years,
> Who knows?

Love may be an empty dream,
Where things are not, tho' they seem,
Love may be an angel's song,
Rising endless, pure and strong,
Who knows?

Hilaire's friendship with Charles Somers Cocks was another that survived his school days.

When he left the Oratory, Hilaire had a touching interview with the then very aged Cardinal Newman. It is plain that the boys knew little about their great and revered Head, for there appears this passage in a letter written by Hilaire the next day: "The Cardinal told me to say many kind things to you from him, and he gave me *The Dream of Gerontius,* a book of his, on leaving. He signed the book 'Newman' in full, and congratulated me on passing with honours the London Matriculation. I believe I am the second who had got honours of all who have matriculated from the Oratory since it began. I think I passed higher than the other." He found out that he had passed 70th out of 793 boys who passed—presumably in the Midlands area of England, as more boys than that would certainly have passed in England as a whole, even before the days of compulsory education.

In later life Hilaire sometimes talked to intimate friends as if he had disliked his school days at the Oratory, yet there is little sign of real unhappiness in any of his letters to Bessie, and I believe she kept them all. But he obviously much preferred the holidays to his school life, in that being unlike certain of his friends.

Before leaving school in 1887, Hilaire wrote a long letter to his mother, who was evidently concerned as to what career he would adopt: "Dearest Mamma, I write this letter for one purpose only, and that a very definite one. I wish you to act upon its information as it is absolutely final. For my profession, *ceteris paribus,* I choose England. I speak English, I wish to write in English. . . . If however I was *driven* by direct pressure to a French profession I should try for one of the great schools, St. Cyr or Fontainebleau. This is all. Keep this letter and act upon it. *I want to live in England. In an English profession I believe I shall gain a place in English writing.* I love my country but I cannot bear the cosmopolitan folly which is destroying the Frank and Gaul in our class. I dislike the life of a Paris student. My desire is to make a name in literature and as I can write in English, I choose England if it be possible. As for which profession, that remains to settle and see which is easiest and best. But *England.* For my country—France, for my patriotism—France; for my society and money and field of work—the country of Minna."

The last word perhaps gives the clue to this impassioned outburst, so at variance with the preferences expressed in earlier letters to Bessie. And less than ten months after writing this letter, he had completely changed his mind—though that change, too, proved to be ephemeral—and in fact Hilaire did ultimately live by the sentiments expressed here. But the tension he felt between his two countries in his early manhood was obviously very deep.

Basil Blackwood and Hilaire Belloc, 1895

Hilaire Belloc, M.P.

Elodie and Louis, their first child

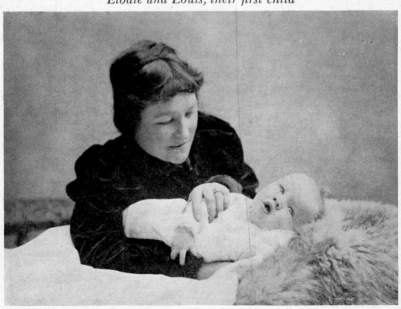

5

AT WAR WITH THE WORLD

→»«←

WHEN Hilaire was seventeen he underwent a complete *volte-face*, and earnestly begged Bessie to allow him to enter the Collège Stanislas with a view to joining the French navy. Various members of our French family regarded this wish as foolish and unreasonable, especially our first cousin, René Millet. I remember a conversation in which he pointed out to Bessie that Hilaire was to all intents and purposes an Englishman and would be neither happy nor successful were he to attempt to turn himself into a Frenchman; moreover our legal guardian, Anatole Dunoyer, who had been a close friend of our father's, told Bessie that he felt certain such an experiment would end in disaster.

Bessie, however, adored France and never forgot—I am tempted to say for a single moment—that we were the children of a Frenchman. I was not surprised when she agreed to Hilaire's wish. Cardinal Newman wrote a fine testimonial to Hilaire's character and abilities, and Father John Norris did the same, but added: "I feel very much his present decision and can't help thinking a safer and more solid career would have opened out to him in this country." Finally, with the reluctant help of Anatole Dunoyer, Hilaire, though past the usual age, was allowed to enter the Collège Stanislas as a student.

What followed had been foreseen by our French relations and should have been obvious to Bessie. Hilaire soon found the life at the French college intolerable after the freedom he had enjoyed at the Oratory which was run on the lines of an English public school owing to the unconscious influence of Cardinal Newman. To give an example: the Oratory boys were free to go into Birmingham unaccompanied by a master, and they were also free to do very much what they liked in their spare time. The pupils of the Collège Stanislas, however, were never allowed to pass through the front door except when accompanied by a man or woman who had been selected by their parents or legal guardians.

The following letter is one of the first we received: "Collège Stanislas, Saturday, Dec. 17th, 1887. Dearest Mamma, if you get to Paris in time today, come and see me at half past four. If you are later it will be of no use. I have leave to go out at half past eleven tomorrow, but you or someone will have to come for me; if you are *at all later than half past eleven* I shall not be able to déjeuner with you, as at that hour the doors are shut and no students are free till twelve, by which time we have lunched. Come then, or send someone at half past eleven sharp, or it will be no use."

Hilaire knew Paris well and had constantly gone in and out of the city from La Celle, so he found this rule extremely irksome. Our guardian, as was natural, undertook to be the official visitor, and he arranged that Hilaire should spend every Sunday and any extra holiday in his apartment on the Ile Saint Louis.

Few letters from this period survive. The following is undated: "We made a pilgrimage to Notre Dame des Victoires on Saturday last, we had to get up at 4.40 A.M. and walk there without food, go to Communion and come back to 'lunch' at eight. We saw the day breaking through the windows of stained glass which was beautiful. They sang the Magnificat— all the little College and all the big College alternately. On the way, Abbé Laurent tried to kill himself. Just opposite the College, in the darkness, a cart knocked him over, and instead of passing over him the wheel dragged him along. He has a hole in his head, but he will probably survive."

There was nothing Hilaire liked about Stanislas, and one day he walked out of the fine old building clad in the distinctive uniform of this famous Paris school. He had saved enough pocket money to pay his fare to England. Well do I recall how he appeared suddenly in our little London house in Great College Street, and almost at once went restlessly off to visit Westminster Abbey. Bessie and I were filled with dismay and apprehension as to what he would decide to do next.

A day later Bessie received a cold but anxious telegram from the Rector of the College saying that Hilaire had disappeared and that a search was being made for him throughout the Paris hospitals as it was feared he had met with an accident. Hilaire declared that nothing would induce him to go back to Paris and Bessie made him write a letter of apology to the Rector. The person who suffered most on account of Hilaire's behaviour was our guardian, Anatole Dunoyer, for the authorities of the College had been unwilling to accept a boy of Hilaire's age and had done so at M. Dunoyer's urgent request. In spite of his dislike of the College—a dislike that persisted all his life—Hilaire's love of France remained the same, and he declared his intention of retaining his French nationality.

Hilaire now announced that he wanted to live in England —but preferably in the country. After much discussion Bessie consulted the Duke of Norfolk's land agent at Arundel, an old and kind acquaintance, and he suggested that Hilaire should work on one of the Duke's farms.

Why, one wonders, were Hilaire's thoughts of a literary career temporarily in abeyance? He had had the encouragement of the publication of *Buzenval* and *Storm* while still a schoolboy. But I have found a letter which perhaps holds the clue we need, which may explain the Stanislas decision as well as the subsequent one to work on a farm: to work with his hands rather than his brain. The letter is dated July 21st, 1887, and it comes from the office of *All the Year Round*—a weekly journal conducted by Charles Dickens' eldest son from 26, Wellington Street, the Strand:

"Dear Madame Belloc, I am sorry that I cannot use any of your son's manuscripts and must return them with many thanks. To be quite frank with you—which, I am sure, will be what you would wish me to be—I do not see anything in them to induce me to give you any other advice about the young man, in connection with a literary career, than I gave you when I had the pleasure of seeing you here the other day. Sincerely yours, Charles Dickens."

Considering Hilaire was six days short of his seventeenth birthday when this letter was written, the discouragement seems strange, and it didn't, in fact, stop him writing poetry as we shall see.

Bessie thought Hilaire would enjoy life on a farm, but I felt certain he would not, and for once I was right. The farmer and his wife both disliked Hilaire and the experiment did not last long. Still, he made a good start, as the following letter will show.

"Manor Farm. Dearest Mamma, I write to you to tell you that the life here is very pleasant. I am surprised at what a farmer calls 'loosing.' There is a man here who is said to be 'loosing.' He has money for house rent, butcher's meat, etc., out of the farm. The rest supports itself and gives him milk and butter and vegetables and the life of a God free man. It is odd that if they cannot give their sons £2,000 to £4,000 to start a farm, they call it 'loosing.' The life is delightful. I get up at six and go to bed at nine. The life is without headwork, it leaves the perceptual brain free, one can smell, hear, taste and think out things with much greater power. Also sleep at night is certain. There is also a great deal of free time. . . . A man here, Sir George Bartlett, said that when there were no landlords, as in France, where the peasants were miserable serfs and lived badly—he was a great fool. The spring is beginning here. I have been blasting wood all morning. . . . I have got my gun. Gun and cover cost four pounds. I have paid for it. Both gun and case are very cheap and according to this farmer very good. I have had a little riding which I like very much."

On Wednesday, August 1st, 1888, when he was just eighteen, Hilaire sent the following poem to Bessie; he said he "found it hard to name" but had called it provisionally "Siren's Song."

> Here are no thoughts but only deep delights,
>   Here all remembrance dies,
> Here never cloud enmists the viewless heights
>   Where the bird lightly flies;
>   And here,
> No ruder sound shall wake thy sleeping ear
> Than the low wind among the trees, that sighs
>   On happy summer nights.
>
> Silent sun-settings upon silent seas
>   Shall rest thee, worn in strife:
> And mornings, glorious in a morning breeze

> Shall stir thy soul to life;
>> Leave then
> The sin-begotten, narrow hopes of men
> The dusty ways where all things vile are rife,
>> For this dear ease.

> Ever amid the laughing waters blue
>> Where the foam murmureth
> And the small wavelets lift them up to woo
>> The passing zephyr's breath
>> Here peace
> Dwells ever. Here rude storms do find surcease
> Here only never come or pain or death,
>> Here only Love is true.

"It is badly executed and hangs loosely," he says in his letter to Bessie. Then: "Have you placed any of my verse yet? Do you think it can be done? They must all be *signed,* and the signature must be Hilaire, not Hilary, Belloc—as I myself sign. I am going to Heron's Ghyll soon and shall need some money. I cannot write short things like *Buzenval* to order; what I write will have my name at the bottom and I do not care to feed people with a spoon, especially if later they are to read me. I am filled with a most gigantic conceit in this respect. If I suppress which, I cannot write with any power. Conceit is the very life of all effort . . . Wish Nurse many happy returns from me and give her my love. Please do not wait to show 'The Office of France' to all the world, but try to get it taken as soon as maybe . . ."

Poor Bessie! But it must be remembered that she herself was a writer and had contacts on all sides in the literary world.

After Hilaire had been on the farm for about six months, he wrote a satirical description of the life he was leading to one of Anatole Dunoyer's sons, including a comic account of the farmer and, what was worse, of the farmer's wife. The couple intercepted the letter which was in French. They had it translated. The result was a melancholy example of the saying that eavesdroppers never hear good of themselves. Already Hilaire had a powerful gift of invective and humour, so the rage of the two people concerned can well be imagined. I went so far as to envisage a libel suit; however, Hilaire had not written anything which could be regarded as libellous though he could express himself very vigorously, both in French and English.

He was asked to leave the farmer's house. He again appeared suddenly and without warning at the house in Great College Street. Again my mother and I anxiously discussed what should be done and what Hilaire would do next. What worried us especially was that at that time we alone seemed to realize his outstanding ability. He had no idea what he wanted to do. In fact he pointed out with something like relief that—as he was French—his call-up papers would soon come for his period of conscription in the French army, so long-term plans could be temporarily postponed.

Hilaire next worked for a short time in an architect's office. He lived, not with Bessie and me, but in lodgings in Bloomsbury. There is a letter dated March 13th, 1889, when he was eighteen: "My work is now draughtmanship. I copy other people's plans; in a few days I shall be laying down original ones from his instructions. At the same time one learns applied mechanics: it is very interesting work, usually one pays a sum to be allowed to do it, but in this case I suppose it pays him to pay his pupil because otherwise he might have to get a regular draughtsman who would be very expensive. . . . All sorts of people have to do with him, among others Tussaud, the son of the wax-modeller. He is very French."

But Hilaire did not stay long in this work. Soon he was working as a journalist and at last—judging by a letter from myself to Bessie—really happy. That he had not been happy before is shown in a letter he wrote later at the time of Cardinal Manning's death to Bessie: "I used to go and see him from my little room in Bloomsbury when I was at war with most of my world. . . ."

At that time I was already writing for the *Pall Mall Gazette* —the remarkable evening paper which published original work by all the outstanding writers of the nineties—and it was through my introduction that Hilaire was given jobs on that paper. I wrote to Bessie who was then in Paris: "Hilary is radiantly happy. He sees more interesting and remarkable people in one morning at the *Pall Mall Gazette* office than he would in six months anywhere else. Mr. Stead is an angel of kindness, he is actually sending him down to Edgbaston all expenses paid to report the Oratory play and breaking up day. . . . I am doing a lot of reviewing. I did 'Ibsen at the Opera Comique' in today's *Pall Mall*."

The only other person I can discover, apart from Mr. Stead, who gave Hilaire real encouragement and help over his literary work was the famous Jesuit priest, Father Mathew Russell, then editor of the *Irish Monthly*. He wrote to my brother from Dublin: "Everything of yours that I have seen has something in it, and please God you will cultivate His gifts humbly and steadily." He goes on to say: "Whom do you address in 'To One Singing'?"

I believe this poem was accepted by Father Mathew.

> Sing ever thus! the Gods themselves shall hear thee,
>   And swear no song was ever so divine
>   As that Titanic hymning, and than thine
> No soul more worthy of its hope; While near thee,
> Coming in this thy strong suspense to cheer thee,

The spirits of thy fathers and of mine
Shall make the sudden sword to leap and shine
For singing thus the Gods themselves might fear thee!

The day of Glory! Lo! the east is red
With its slow dawning; and I see the lance
And helm and steel that erst the Maiden led
I see the Past in terrible advance.
The Marseillaise has woken up the dead
Hail! to the coming! Hail! to thee, my France!

In October 1890, when Hilaire was just twenty there appeared his first literary venture, a monthly magazine called *The Paternoster Review*. He took an office at 11, Clement's Inn, the Strand, and at first the prospects were encouraging. Writing to Bessie in September he says: "Just a line to acknowledge your letter. We are having a great success—£60 of advertisements already! We are getting 6 guineas a page all round—quite beyond what we expected. Our first number is very strong—I have just rushed over to Ireland and back. You will get the first number on the 26th."

Various friends including James Hope put money into *The Paternoster,* and both Bessie and myself worked hard in obtaining subscribers. The first list of subscribers and contributors contain among others the following names: Cardinal Manning, the Duke of Norfolk, Coventry Patmore, Aubrey de Vere, Professor St. George Mivart, Canon Farrar, F. C. Burnand, the Editor of *Punch* and W. T. Stead, the editor of *The Pall Mall Gazette.*

Hilaire wrote a short catechism by way of advertisement:

Q. What is *The Paternoster Review?*
A. It is a magazine started by a number of people who are sick of those perpetual morbid and loose articles in so many of the modern reviews.

Q. Do you mean that there is to be religious propaganda carried on in it?

A. On the contrary. It is going to rigidly exclude *all* articles which touch on Religion or Morals.

Q. But why?

A. Because it is in the very spirit of the thing to treat all questions on common Christian truths or morals as settled and closed.

Q. What sort of articles is it going to have?

A. In the choice of its articles the Managers will be guided chiefly by the topical interest of the moment and by the literary excellence of purely literary matter. For instance, Africa is in the air, and they have secured articles on its divisions by the best men.

Q. But they will have to pay high?

A. They do pay high.

Q. And they will have to admit new men sometimes?

A. It is a principle of theirs to admit new men and foreign writers as a good feature.

Q. What do they sell at?

A. Sixpence a month. Eight shillings a year post free. To all those who comprehend our motto, 'Fate fights for those who dare.' We feel that the time when all men of honesty will have to stand shoulder to shoulder is not far distant; is possibly close at hand. As to our youth, it only makes us the more hopeful with regard to the issue of the battle.

As a result of *The Paternoster Review,* Hilaire met most of the literary men of his day. Wilfrid Blunt wrote a charming letter to this unknown young man, and the friendship thus begun lasted till Blunt's death. In the second number George Meredith contributed a striking poem called "The Riddle for Men," and the newspapers and magazines both in England and Ireland wrote welcoming notices. To Hilaire's surprise, *The Paternoster Review* together with *The Nineteenth Cen-*

tury was publicly burnt in Turkey as a result of an article on Armenia. I must confess I was not surprised.

I do not know how many numbers of the review appeared. I possess none after the issue of January 1891, which contains an article by Cardinal Manning on General Booth's work as described in *Darkest England*. Manning writes: "Let him try his hand, and if he fail let others do better. Above all it is intolerable to hinder General Booth in feeding the starving and reclaiming the criminal of this day because in the next generation a normal state of capital and labour may provide employment for posterity. In the meanwhile, must they starve?"

I'm afraid it was a bitter blow to Hilaire's pride when *The Paternoster Review* had to cease publication. In my view it would have had a chance of survival had there been behind it a good man of business. This, however, was not the case. To Bessie's distress, and Hilaire's mortification, the money which had been put up by various friends was lost. The numbers that did appear must be rare specimens of Victoriana.

It was at this time that Hilaire first met Elodie, who later became his wife. She with her mother, Mrs. Hogan, and her sister, Elizabeth, were touring Europe. They had been to Rome and were now in London before returning to California. Hilaire thought that the introduction to us had been effected by Mr. W. T. Stead, but Bessie believed it was a priest in Rome who had introduced us.

Mrs. Hogan intended to stay in London for at least a month, but she received a telegram saying that one of her sons was ill; the news alarmed her and she decided to go straight back to America. Elodie and Elizabeth were deeply disappointed at the thought of leaving Europe before they had become acquainted with London, so my mother, who had taken a great liking to them, suggested that they should spend a month with us in our house in Great College Street.

We had let the two ground-floor rooms of the house, a sitting-room and a bedroom, to a friend and fellow writer named Margaret Curtoise. I seldom saw Miss Curtoise; though I was truly attached to her, we had little in common apart from a love of literature. She was at least twenty years older than I was. However she filled the role of an invisible chaperone, for my mother would not have allowed me to live there by myself while she was either in Sussex or in France, as was constantly the case.

Miss Curtoise happened just then to be away, and I wrote and asked her whether she would allow us to rent the rooms back for a little while, so as to entertain our young American friends. She consented, and Elizabeth and Elodie arrived. I was myself working very hard, and though not actually on the staff of *The Pall Mall Gazette,* I was an almost daily contributor. I was also beginning to write for other papers.

Both Elodie and Elizabeth were deeply religious; they went to Mass every day, at the old Jesuit Church in Horseferry Road, and I remember feeling slightly surprised when I learned that my brother frequently came down from his Bloomsbury lodgings and went with them. After a happy and interesting month of sightseeing, and of making acquaintance with many of our friends, all of whom were bewitched by the charm of the younger sister, and by the ability of the elder, Elodie and Elizabeth returned to America.

Although my brother had been "showing them the sights of London," as one of them expressed it in a letter she wrote to our mother soon after her return to California, it was not apparent that he was seriously attracted to either sister. We were much moved by a letter from Elodie which came to us in which she wrote of "an undying remembrance of all the

love and kindness and sweetness which you both gave to us
. . . strangers whom you took in, whom you sheltered, and
to whom you gave unquestionable love and friendship. Ah,
dearest Madame Belloc and Marie, we shall only be dust
when we forget you."

Elodie, on her return to America, intended to join the Sisters of Charity. Her mother not only approved but eagerly
wished her to do so.

I, meanwhile, was absorbed in my new life of writing. I felt
both Elodie and Elizabeth were more my mother's friends
than mine, though I liked them both, and realized that they
were exceptionally clever girls. The two sisters, though extremely different, were devoted to one another. Elizabeth was
plain and powerful looking; Elodie was graceful, with a remarkably pretty figure. She had a very white skin, and her
hair was of the red gold tint which occasionally but by no
means always, is seen with that complexion. She was well read
and had begun to write and had contributed to one of the
Catholic magazines. I remember an article of hers on the old
Spanish settlements in California.

My brother fell in love with Elodie at first sight, which is
shown by a letter he wrote to a friend very soon after he had
first seen her, but I was not aware of the deep impression she
had made on him. Shortly after the two sisters had left London, Mrs. Rundle Charles, at this time my mother's closest
friend, was asked by Hilaire to lend him enough money to go
steerage to America. He explained to her that he had fallen
in love with Elodie Hogan, and that he felt certain she had
not got a vocation for the religious life. He declared he wished
to enter, were she willing, into an informal engagement.

Mrs. Rundle Charles lent him a small sum, and he raised
the balance of the passage money by selling the prizes he had
won at the Oratory School. They were of added value as each

bore the signature of Cardinal Newman. After Hilaire had sailed a friend saw the books on sale at a shop in Oxford Street, and she told my mother. Bessie immediately went and bought them back, as she knew how much her son valued them.

Hilaire was fond of travelling, and he had already made long expeditions into various parts of Europe whenever he had earned enough money to do so. He told my mother that he intended to go to America to visit our Priestley relations, and to see the country. So little did she realize what else he had in mind that I was thunderstruck when later on my mother told me she had received a letter from Elodie's mother, stating Hilaire was arriving in California with a view to asking Elodie to marry him. She went on to say Elodie was about to enter a convent, as she had a vocation, and had long wished to be a nun. Mrs. Hogan strongly disapproved of Hilaire from every point of view, but she very rightly in my opinion allowed him to see her daughter before he left America.

This is the first letter we received after he had sailed: "Dearest Mamma, just a line to tell you that I have got to Queenstown quite safely. The Welsh mountains are very grand from the sea and curiously enough one sees them at once from Liverpool. This is, I believe, the same boat as that in which the Misses Hogan crossed—it is a very good one. The sea is not remarkably rough either, but the strong shaking of the screw makes writing very difficult. Squinting down at the saloons they seem to me rather tawdry; the photos, of course, make them out gorgeous to a degree, but they are a fraud."

He reached Brooklyn in February, 1891. "Dearest Mamma, I came here quite safely yesterday after a voyage that was fairly comfortable but rather stormy. This town is excessively ugly, built of bright red brick with very narrow streets and tall houses most of them in the style of the big buildings past St. James's Station. The Brooklyn Bridge is very fine and the Bartholdi Statue of Liberty is like a French cook in a foreign country, being immeasurably good in the middle of what is immeasurably bad. All over it inside there are directions for putting it together in French. The harbour is the finest I have ever seen. I go on to the Priestleys on Thursday. I shall have ample money to get to California where I expect your reply. The common people here are wonderfully honest and independent. And they are as polite to other citizens as are the French themselves. New York is as far south as *Madrid*—think of it! And Philadelphia almost as far south as Algiers. . . . Seven days at sea is a very very long time. The old men officials and soldiers are just like the French in face—hard dark skins, crisp hair and square faces. The food is cheap and admirable."

From Philadelphia in March he wrote: "Nothing is more remarkable in this country than the individual nationality of the people. In manner and habits they resemble the French perhaps more than any other, and they are as unlike the English as any nation can be. This has been caused, I fancy, by the fact that all the emigrants to the United States for a hundred years must have been men peculiarly different in political ideas and in temperament from the mass of Englishmen. They are quite as broad in conversation as the French are, and this has a most peculiar effect upon an English ear in the English tongue. Moreover, there is *no lower class*—absolutely none. No difference in tone can be distinguished between the address of a Negro servant and of a friend—both are polite to a degree. . . . They have here two libraries less complete than the British Museum but infinitely better managed and free to all the world—a very wonderful place."

He stopped at Grand Junction, Colorado. "You will find this place in the east of the State, about half way between north and south. All the mountains have become confused to me, they are 1,500 miles broad! And between the ranges nothing but deserts of sand. I am earning a little money. . . ."

Hilaire reached San Francisco on March 10th. "California is a fruitful valley between two ranges of mountains, the people are absolutely French in all their manners, and equality is absolute too. They drink wine, which is necessary to salvation, swear continually, are healthy in mind, chivalrous and brave. No country is so made for the future, none so republican, a little time and they will have great artists and poets: and Elodie is here—worth many journeys."

At last Hilaire had reached the goal of his journey. Mrs. Hogan received him with kindness, and as I have said she allowed him to see Elodie for a short time before she went off to stay with a married sister, and it was from there she must have written her answer to Hilaire who by that time had returned East.

"Montclair, New Jersey, April 30th, 1891. My dearest Mother, Elodie's refusal came today. It is very final and definite and I must accept it. I shall in all probability leave this country for England next Wednesday, May 6, getting to London on May 15. You must be a good friend to me, for I have been hit very hard indeed, harder than I thought I could be hit—and you are evidently the best friend I have. I shall want to go to the country when I get back to England. Perhaps you can come with me? I have answered Elodie. Your affectionate son, Hilaire Belloc."

Bessie was deeply distressed by Hilaire's state of mind when he returned to England. So much so that on October 2nd, 1891, she wrote to Elodie from La Celle Saint Cloud influenced, perhaps, by poignant recollections of her own happy married life:

"Dearest Elodie, will you cross the Atlantic and come and see me quietly at Slindon? Hilary goes to his military service about the 10th of November. I have already told you more than eight months ago that I only desire to know what is really in your mind; and if you love my son, you certainly ought not to enter the religious life. Any reasonable priest, indeed *any* priest, would tell you the same. There is nothing wrong in your love for each other, and I cannot in the least understand the misery which you cause the one to the other. Pray, my dear child, do not waste your life and his, in a struggle of feeling which seems to me quite wrong and useless, and if you do love him, follow the love simply, as God's will, and come over to me. Yours ever affectionately, Bessie R. Belloc. Hilary will probably serve his year in the East of France. He will have four days holiday at the New Year."

I do not know if Elodie answered this noble letter—I call it noble, as Hilaire was only twenty-one at the time and had no income on which to keep a wife. It seems obvious, looking back, that Elodie was undecided as to where her future happiness lay and wanted, if possible, to keep all doors open.

6

MEN OF A GUN

→»«←

H ILAIRE RECEIVED his *feuille d'appel* on the 9th of November, 1891, when he was twenty-one. All the members of our family in France, and especially René Millet, took a deep interest in my brother's military service. René suggested that he should be posted to a regiment stationed at Versailles so as to be within three miles of our home at La Celle. Hilaire, however, rejected this idea and, to the amazement of everyone, said he would rather serve in the distant garrison of Toul close to the German frontier. Bessie was much distressed at this decision, for she was afraid his health would suffer, as the training of the French conscript of those days was indeed Spartan.

Before going to Toul, Hilaire spent a few days by himself at La Celle where he chose to sleep in the then empty Châlet —the house where Bessie had passed her brief happy married life and where Louis had died. But Hilaire was driven out by the cold—on November 10th he wrote: "Last night it froze 14 degrees Fahrenheit."

Those of our French family who were at La Celle welcomed him warmly though they all regarded his desire to serve on the frontier with disapproval; they would have preferred him to be in the cavalry as he was fond of riding. But this was not possible. "Paul Deroulède was greatly pleased at my going into the army, but he has no great affection for the artillery. However, I could not have chosen the cavalry as only three-year conscripts are put into it."

Far from serving for three years, Hilaire, as the only son of a widow, could claim a *dispensation* by which he need serve for only one year. Very early in his military service he began worrying about this: "The officers tell me that I must *reclamer* constantly and not let time pass, so whatever effort lays to your hand had better be tried several times, and soon. A Breton under my circumstances recently succeeded in the same thing here—only his *dispense* was less urgent than mine. . . . Write often. Your loving son, Hilaire Belloc."

He wrote detailed descriptions of his life. "November 20th, 1891. 10th Battery of the 8th Regiment of Artillery, Toul, Meurthe-et-Moselle. . . . I would have written before but my time is exceedingly full. From half-past five in the morning till five at night one's time is entirely taken up and there is not a moment to spend as one would. From five to nine in the evening one is not taken for any service, but one has so much to clean that even then one has little time. On the whole this does not weigh much because the day is varied and passes very quickly. The discipline is extremely strict and the punctuality extreme. The rigidity required for one's ordinary duties makes many things easy which would be impossible in civil life. There are men sent here from the centre every year, but never men from here to the centre, so that the frontier is constantly reinforced. There are 7,000 civilians in Toul, men, women and children, but there are 13,000 soldiers, so that for every adult man in Toul there are at least six soldiers. . . . Tomorrow there will be a review before the General commanding the artillery of the *Corps d'Armée*. It would be very fine if the weather were better, but I have never seen anything so bad since I passed through Nebraska a year ago."

For much of the time his thoughts were anywhere but in Toul. In one of his letters he told us that Elodie's brother, John Hogan, was in England working with a tutor in Cambridge and he asked us to try to find out the address and "do him some kindness. . . . He is my link with California, and can tell me if things are going well." And on another occasion: "I have got a very affectionate letter from Father John, together with a new magazine started at the Oratory! He wants me to write for it, and I must try and find time to do so. He is very complimentary to me in his letter and speaks a great deal about religion, which is odd from him."

He was issued with his uniforms in the middle of November. He described the full dress as "black with red stripes and facings, and a big sword. . . . Do not fret after me, for I do not look on this as an evil. Evils are not material—I for my part have a great pride in wearing the uniform, for the patriotism which you may have thought affected is one of the strongest feelings I have. I think you exaggerate my indifference to the various emotions of a man. . . . I find no difficulty with the men, they are all Frenchmen of different rank, but in my *pièce,* which is the same as my room, as all the men of a gun sleep together, they are all of the artisan class." He reassured Bessie as to food, which he declared to be "good, and it can be eaten easily," but he admitted that it was "very coarse." But he was always preoccupied about his *dispensation.* He often underlined what he wrote in letters and soon there came: *"Whatever is done about my one year's service should be done as soon as possible, and continually repeated. . . .* Three years would be a terrible break in my life. But I think you know this."

Hilaire's letters came frequently: ". . . Next Friday,

Decm. 4th, is the Ste. Barbe, the feast of the artillery; all the French artillery treat it like a Sunday, with special leave, etc; but there are many expenses on that day especially for the new soldiers—we are supposed to contribute something to the regimental dinner which is given on that day. I would therefore be a great deal relieved if you could send me 50 francs so as to get to me on the 3rd of December. . . . Are there any letters from America? Post them on at once if there are." But to Bessie's childlike surprise, unregistered money orders failed to reach him, and he begged her most earnestly to register any letter containing money.

"It would give me great pleasure if you could afford to come to Toul in December, perhaps you will think it too near the New Year. . . . Now that the recruit drill is coming to an end one can get short leaves of Saturday or Sunday night and go to Nancy or the hills up country—a blessing which no one can understand who has not lived tied up with the tremendous work of a frontier garrison. You speak of coming to Paris. . . . I wonder so much if you could come to Toul. If you came on a *Saturday* I could get the whole of Saturday afternoon and Sunday till Monday morning roll call; they always give 24 hours to a man whose parents come to the town —a word to me that you were coming would suffice. Could you do it without too much fatigue or expense? It would do me good to see you again, and beyond my leave I could see you always between 5 and 9 on ordinary days. Do you think you could manage it? If you could pray let me know by return. . . . I am afraid the journey will seem very long but it would be a blessing to me if you could come."

He had an alternative plan of perhaps being able to get to Paris—it was possible to get there and back in a day. "I am keen to see you again and also our native hills and the Seine. I had a wonderful glimpse of the Cathedral and the Gothic roofs by moonlight just now, from an *open* staircase under a great old roof of a house where one of the soldiers has a room. One thinks of oneself as in 1400, but one is here in an iron system, on a frontier trained for a terrible modern war . . ." And then comes almost the only complaint I have found in his letters: "Think of me often, for the life is the last limit of hardship—with the uniform to counterbalance it."

So anxious was Bessie concerning Hilaire's health that she answered his appeal and travelled to Toul, but not before March. She experienced fearful weather and it snowed for two days. During one snowstorm the men manoeuvred from three o'clock to five.

During January, 1892, Hilaire wrote with deep feeling of the death of Cardinal Manning: "It has given me a great shock. Of course he was certain to die sooner or later; he was so old and feeble—but I would have liked to see him again before he died. He was always very sympathetic to me." He said that he had written some verses "to the poor" in the Cardinal's memory, and hoped they would be printed in the Oratory School magazine.

In this same letter he added: "I wish you would write oftener; none of my friends write to me, and I have no news from America which is very terrible to me. It was yesterday a year ago that Elodie wrote me the letter which took me to California." It was fortunate indeed that he had fallen in love with his future wife; she was ever in his thoughts, and in many letters which he wrote to his mother he mentioned Elodie.

A poem published in a newspaper a year after his service was over may have been written at this time. It contains a hint of the nostalgic magic of such lyrics as "Do you Remember an Inn, Miranda?" It is called *"En Bivouac"*:

You came without a human sound
You came and brought my soul to me;
I only woke, and all around
They slumbered on the firelit ground
Beside the guns of Burgundy.

I felt the gesture of your hands,
You signed my forehead with the cross:
The gesture of your holy hands
Was bounteous—like the misty lands
Among the hills in Calvados.

But when I slept I saw your eyes,
Hungry as death, and very far.
I saw demand in your dim eyes
Mysterious as the moons that rise
At midnight, in the pines of Var.

It was a very hard spring—as the snow in March at the time of Bessie's visit shows. Hilaire wrote: "We passed full privates yesterday and defiled before the Colonel. It is very striking to see all the men here passing in column with music and the swords at Present Arms. The review on horseback comes on in a day or two. . . . The parts of the life which are pleasant are above all the physical ones, but there are days when the fatigue is very great, it tells on the head more than the body—preventing one's sleep. . . . I took stable guard, which involves twenty hours of work to four hours of sleep and I had service in the snow which gave me a bad sore throat. The days are very long in one's bed looking at the ceiling. I have nothing to read. . . ."

Boredom was another ordeal to be faced. He begged for English books, and arranged with a tradesman in Toul to receive parcels addressed to him. "And I very much want to see *The Lamp* if you could send me the number of the last two months, I should be so happy. You know there is work of mine in it. Also I must write to Father John to get the Oratory School Magazine. . . . When you have read a literary paper like the *Figaro*—please pass it on."

I am afraid Hilaire was very short of money. I remember sending him 20 francs and some eatables, and he said the money would help him to pay a pork-butcher's bill, while he had spread the meat I sent on some bread—"it makes more food."

In April, 1892, came the following: "This is the hardest time in the year. The mobilization has begun and we are very hard driven. Two days ago we had to get up at one o'clock in the morning and start off for Nancy at three. We had slept three hours and we had to get everything ready in two hours and the whole lot started off two hours before dawn—six hundred horses, eight hundred men and thirty-six cannon. It was a very fine sight indeed. The column was nearly a mile long. The sun rose while we were in the great forest of La Haye. There, in the plateau above the town, we made coffee. It was ten o'clock by the time we ate, and we had done the distance on nothing. We manoeuvred with the infantry which joined us from Nancy and came back about three o'clock in the evening.

"I had no leave at Easter. A certain number always stay behind to look after the horses. . . . I got to Mass on Easter Sunday at St. Genhoult, the old church where my captain goes [Bessie had written a few weeks before "Do try to get to Mass on Sundays. It is a great distress to me to think you are hindered from going"]. Hilaire continues: "We have an embarcation on the 10th of May, all the battery horses, men and cannon are put into a train. It takes two hours. We have already had our orders. It is hard work, as it has to be done in the middle of the night. The horses are packed like sardines, and object very much to moving in. . . . I am with the horses because I am a driver. The train does not move, it is only to see how soon it is got over that they do it. . . . I went to Verdun on Sunday night leave. It is like Arundel, pitched on a rock over the Moselle, before it joins the Meurthe. The woods are in a horseshoe and very grand. The streets are so steep that there are *no horses* in the town."

What Hilaire seems to have really enjoyed at Toul was the riding. "We are already riding every kind of horse," he wrote, "without stirrups—jumping and getting on and off at the gallop. They teach the men very thoroughly here." He described an interesting and exciting experience when he rode with two horses at once for the first time. "The whole art lies in getting the horse you ride and the horse you lead to act as one. It would be impossible but for the rigorous training one has received. The men are taught to jump off and on at the gallop until they are one with the beast they ride. My riding horse is called Boussole, brown with a white nose and very frisky. My led horse is called Bastiglione and is just like the horse in the Heliodorus of Raphael, of which you have the head in the crayon sketches at home."

". . . I was guard at the Horse Infirmary—one does nothing there but feed the horses that are ill, so I had all the twenty-four hours to myself on the straw. There is a mare with a little colt who is very funny. He got loose in the middle of the night and I woke up to see him staring at me. I got up and tied him fast again at 2 in the morning. When the veterinary surgeon comes round in the morning the horses hobble and cough and hang their heads, just like men who play at being sick to escape service . . ."

". . . There has come a new General, General de St. Germain, to command the garrison. He is promoted from Nice which may interest you. There was a hedge of infantry in *terre de campagne* for a mile and a half to receive him, all the music and 150 of our men on horseback as an escort, the rest with the guns lining the road. A very grand sight indeed, a hollow square in front of the Cathedral where the General's Palace is. He will probably bother us with a mobilization in a day or two, to see how ready we are, and I shall hear the long sad notes of the *Générale* in the middle of the night calling all the men up—a very grand but very trying experience, a mobilization. . . . We are all looking forward to the camp in six weeks where is all the fun of campaigning without any of the garrison trouble."

Nurse Mew remained until her death an important figure in our lives. She wrote constantly to Hilaire, and he appreciated this. "I am very much touched by Nurse's letter. It is so touching to get a letter ill-spelt and without stops, and yet so full of feeling. She has a wonderful character—it is people like that who make the strength of England."

The bright spots in Hilaire's life were his leaves—or the expectation of them—which came at Carnival time or on special feastdays: "I believe I shall have leave to go to Paris for a short day or perhaps even to Luxembourg"—where the Dutreux were at the time. But what really eased his mind was when he knew definitely that his service would last only one year instead of three. The *dispense* was finally obtained through the intercession of René Millet, after Hilaire had finally consented to Bessie's writing to him for help.

Bessie wrote to Hilaire: "I had hoped to be the first to tell you that you are let off with one year of military service. René wrote to London. I was afraid of some mistake which might prove a great disappointment if I wrote prematurely. I con-

gratulate you, my darling, for I thought Toul very dreary.
. . ." She was writing this from Beaulieu where she was staying with her American friend Mrs. Kelsey, and goes on: "I
thought of you the other day while I was looking at the sea of
Ulysses, in a sharp breeze and foam curling on all the waves.
I particularly want you to see it first with me. I have many
delightful associations with the Mediterranean."

Hilaire wrote happier letters once he knew his *dispensation*
had been obtained, and summer was coming and he was on
the move. "We are on the march to Châlons at the third stage
—Révigny—a very curious old town. We shall be in camp
Saturday next."

"*Camp de Chalons, 8ème Régiment d'Artillerie, 10ème
Batterie, Juillet 10, 1892. Dimanche.* . . . We came in an
hour or two ago after a seven days' march. We marched by
way of Commercy and Bar-le-Duc but did not pass the Châlons road, we skirted north. The camp is an immense heath
fifteen miles every way. Very flat with small pine woods about
it. Where we are—in the extreme north of the camp—we are
close to the Hill of Reims. I hope next week to get to Reims,
a town of which I am very fond. It is very fine and striking
here, two regiments of men with 144 cannon and 16 or 17
hundred horse, all under canvas or the open sky, with the immense forest hills of Reims close to the North and the huge
plain of the Pouilleux going south to the Marne. From the
least height one sees miles and miles—that is why it has been
chosen for artillery practice. We fire at targets six or seven
kilometres off, or sometimes nearer, at four to three. We have
to get up very early. Do you know that during the whole of
the march I had to get up at half past two every day? At half
past three we started and marched right on till nine or ten,
with short halts every hour. The heat is terrible—the tents
are boiling; there are ten men to a tent—just room to dress

by turns. But the nights are cool and one wakes up in the early morning quite refreshed. I am in a kind of sack, on the top of a bundle of straw, and a rough coverlet called a *campement* over me—all the regulations are the same as in manoeuvres or war, hence we get a little better food which is a blessing."

And a few days later. "The heat is awful. Three regiments of artillery have come for the manoeuvres and everything is getting hotter and dustier every hour. We shall have several thousand men concentrated and there is trouble in watering them and their horses. They have been forced to give two days complete rest, as a third of the battery fell off service with the heat. . . . Mind you send me all Election news—do not send me too many papers, say two or three a week, but let me know the results when they come in; up to now I am sincerely surprised to see what large returns comparatively the Conservatives are getting—I suppose I have enough enthusiasm left to hope for a Liberal victory, but I have lost a great deal of my splendid illusions. I have, I do not know where in my nature, a crying mercy for the very poor—but the Conservatives have at least all the cynics, and you know that cynics are the only people who ever give a penny to a beggar. If the Liberals drive out music at last, as they have already driven out good art and good wine and common sense, I suppose I shall say I am Tory—but I have been so Radical!"

Here we have at last the authentic Hilaire Belloc, the man known to the world—born of tensions and experiences and thought undergone chiefly in Bloomsbury, the United States, and now in Toul. He was just on twenty-two. "Do not forget that it is my birthday on the 27th, and that I am your son who has been by statute a French citizen for a whole year, and who is sweltering away like a convict under canvas at the beck and call of everybody—for an idea."

"July 31st, 1892. Dearest Mamma, thank you so much for the fifty francs you and Mary sent for my birthday. It enabled me to get to Paris for 24 hours which is, in this kind of life, a greater pleasure than you can know. I have been six months and a half without a single respite from quarters except when you came, and the day I walked over to Avenay. . . ."

As the year of Hilaire's military service drew to a close, his cousin, René Millet, suggested that he should apply to become an interpreter in the French army. This Hilaire entirely refused to consider:

He wrote to Bessie on August 15th: "As to the interpreter scheme I would not dream of such a life as a permanency. My whole ambition is in politics and letters. I prefer infinitely to be earning little and to be in London and Paris in the centre of learning and living. I would *immensely* like to voyage free for a short time, a year or two, but I would shrink from anything definite or professional about it. I know you think I can earn no money in the great centres, but I am getting older and learning many things. . . . I have read the *Mariage de Loti* on stable guard between snatches of sleep and dreaming, and it brought back California to me very vividly. If it were not getting too dark to see my pen, I should write you a whole page of psychology. The camp life is over, and in another month I shall be on my own legs. I will take any position in London to form a nucleus from which I can write on the papers that know me. I kiss you very fondly as French boys kiss their mothers, only my life has had much more of trouble and drama than theirs. Always your son, Hilaire Belloc."

Another idea for Hilaire's immediate future came through my intervention. It was that he should go to Oxford. I shall explain how the idea came about in the next chapter, but I quote here Hilaire's reaction to it as it appears in his next letter. Bessie, in writing to suggest Oxford to him, evidently feared a negative reply.

"As to Oxford, I shall certainly jump at it. I am afraid you have misunderstood my gadding about the world. I have two or three principles which I would not change. I had, in California, what a call is to other men, and what I would have died for! And in my service of France an equally sacred idea which I have kept to and played out to what is practically the end—unless there should be a war. The classics, and the society of my equals, is just what I now most desire. The only thing that opposed them was, quite simply, my poverty. I had to keep free, the only other alternative was subordination to a commercial standard which put me out. I do not understand the rules by which men cheat each other with impunity in a modern state. . . . From what James Hope has told me one can get on quite well at Oxford on the sum you have named and I shall have—not only leisure to write but the opportunity in which I can write infinitely better than in the hard life I led in London, so pray accept the offer. Oxford is a turning point from which there are many roads. . . . I think Hope stays on another year. Anyhow I know at least a dozen men at Oxford—Lord Ashbourne's son, whom Westmeath converted, Westmeath himself, and several others. I am exercised about the *matriculation* for Oxford. One does not enter as into a public school. The necessity for immediate action is that if I find London matriculation with honours admits me, I need not work; whereas if it does not I must come back to London immediately and begin to work, after a week or so with Madame Dutreux."

Hilaire's last long letter from the French army gives his views on the effects of the three-year service: "I will give a friend of mine here, a medical student, the charge of paying

my very few bills. I cannot go into town myself as I am confined to barracks three days. Nominally because my horse was
dirty, but in reality I fancy because I have not lent money to
my *sergent.* . . . A gentleman who wishes to be a French
soldier and neither to fall ill, nor to be continually punished
should have to nourish himself every day and pay his 'chop'
into the bargain, and as my fortune did not permit this, I have
seen a good deal of suffering here for you know, when I have
got something into my head the *idée fixe* prevents my giving
way. The effect of three years' military service will be to bring
back a strong upper hand in France. The professional, and
highly-connected class will form an aristocracy and will take
care to hold the power inevitably—the oligarchy you have
come to in England by national means, has come to us by
terrible experience, but the mob will never have the cannon
again in France because the ruling class know the value of
cannon now. The men of the upper class who have seen the
people close in the service and who have there appreciated
the value of arms are still quite young, but the first of them
are beginning to hold power."

Then comes a brief note: "Dearest Mamma. Just a line in
great haste. I leave *Saturday 18th*. A new order. Pray see that
my clothes come at least by the 16th. Otherwise I am in a bad
fix as the one-year men may not leave in uniform. Please have
them sent by the very quickest manner. I must go to La Celle
at once to get my pass viewed by the *gendarmerie,* it is a thing
one has to have done—the day after one's liberation, under
pain of all sorts of difficulty. So I *must* go to Bougival on the
19th. . . . Pray attend to this. I have learnt the news just now
and the post is starting."

Hilaire, while still a young man, would now and then give
a lecture on his life in the French army. I was never present,

but I have met several people who were, and I used to smile to myself at the delightful impression left on their minds by my brother's words. Many years later in his dedication of *Avril,* a book of essays on French Renaissance poetry, he wrote: "I can put to my credit a year of active, if eccentric, experience in a French barrack room, and complete segregation during those twelve memorable months wherein I could study the very soul of this sincere, creative and tenacious people."

These letters from Hilaire Belloc tell the story of his year's service in the French army better than any words of mine. Bessie to the end of her long life kept them in a little packet on her writing-table. I do not believe she ever re-read them, but she often held them in her beautiful hands (the one physical attribute her only son inherited from her) while she spoke to me of that year of Hilaire's life.

7

THE BALLIOL DEMOSTHENES

-»>×«<-

WHILE Hilaire was serving in the French army I was living
in London making new friends, and working hard on the
Pall Mall Gazette under its famous editor, W. T. Stead. I had
already published a biography of Charlotte Elizabeth, Princess Palatine, and I think this must have impressed Mr. Stead
for he allowed me to come and go in his office as I wished,
taught me with great patience how to write newspaper articles
and edit paragraphs, and put some work in my way. But as
he was an extremely busy man he selected a member of his
staff to help look after me. This was Edmund Garrett—the
first Englishman I knew really well.

I have wondered since how Edmund Garrett drifted into
journalism, and especially into the very trying form of evening paper journalism. He was not strong, yet had to be at
the office very early in the morning. We became friends,
though I do not remember that Edmund Garrett was interested, as I was, in literature. He had political ambitions and
was an ardent Liberal. He had advanced views concerning the
rights of women, which pleased me: in that at least we saw
eye to eye. For the first time since the death of my English

grandmother I felt happy in England. Everything interested me—literature, art and politics.

My mother's friends, however "advanced" they may have been when they were young, were conventional people and were surprised at the free life I led once I started earning my living. In those days no English girl would have gone unchaperoned to a young man's rooms; yet I went to Edmund Garrett's rooms near the British Museum, and there met young men who thought me as unusual as I am sure he did. He took me to visit two maiden cousins who had heard of my behaviour and were worried—afraid, doubtless, that Edmund would fall in love with me. The visit was not a success. He asked me afterwards what I had thought of the way his cousins dressed, as he had noticed that I dressed fashionably and usually brought new clothes back from Paris when I went there to collect material for *Pall Mall* articles, whereas his cousins wore smocked dresses made from stuff that recalled Morris wall-papers. I told him, after putting up some resistance, that I found his cousins' clothes hideous and that in my opinion everyone ought to dress in the fashion. He wrote me a long letter pointing out that this view was to him utterly degraded and most astonishing on the part of the kind of person he had supposed me to be.

Edmund Garrett had a contempt for the girl who stayed at home waiting to be married. He admired and respected young women who worked. In those days there were not many, but I was one of them. Being a French girl I took it for granted that I would marry some day. At that time in the world's history there was hardly such a thing as an unmarried Frenchwoman. The French girl either married or became a nun—unless it was her active wish to remain single, as was the case with Mademoiselle de Montgolfier.

But Edmund Garrett was not the only man I met through

the *Pall Mall Gazette*. Grant Richards also worked in the office, a clever young man, a little younger than myself, who shared my intense interest in contemporary literature. We quickly became friends, and it was through him that I met my future husband and the man who was instrumental in helping Hilaire to get to Oxford.

Grant Richards, whose father was a distinguished don, asked his mother to invite me to Oxford for Eights Week. Though Bessie disliked my paying visits without her, she finally consented to allow me to accept the invitation, and I bought two pairs of shoes and had made a pale pink cotton frock. I look back on that week as one of the happiest in my life, for everything about Oxford enchanted me; moreover I became an ordinary girl again, for none of the undergraduates I met knew that I was a writer. Grant Richards' parents lived in Beaumont Street and entertained a good deal. One afternoon three young men came to call on Mrs. Richards. One was Laurence Binyon, one was Mr. Thornton who in time became a distinguished medical man, and the third was an undergraduate at Trinity called Frederic Lowndes. Frederic Lowndes, apparently, decided to marry me as soon as he entered the room.

He saw as much of me as he could during the days that followed and somehow contrived to travel back to London with me. I presume he tipped the guard to see that no one else got into the carriage, for when we were alone he asked me to marry him. I was much taken aback and told him that I considered myself, if not engaged, at least bound to someone who was then in the West Indies. He asked me if we could go on being friends and I agreed.

He at once began to write to me and must certainly have gained my trust, for soon I was telling him all about my anxiety concerning Hilaire's future once he left the French army.

In return he suggested that Hilaire should try to obtain an Oxford scholarship. I was entirely ignorant of all that side of English life, but this suggestion seemed to me admirable and caused me to think out a scheme which I imparted to Bessie who, to my surprise and relief, raised no serious objection. The fact was that she, too, realized that very soon Hilaire's future would present a serious problem; and whatever other people thought of him, my mother and I knew he was extremely clever, with a strong, determined type of mind. Frederic Lowndes, too, as soon as he met Hilaire, perceived his exceptional ability. Apart from his brains, he was so full of vitality—indeed I have never known any young man so highly vitalized as was Hilaire at that time.

Pursuing my plan, I wrote the following letter from Great College Street: "Dear Mr. Lowndes, you will say to yourself that this is too much of a good thing, but if you can spare the time I want you to be kind enough to answer me the following questions. Is £200 a year enough for a young man to be fairly comfortable at Oxford? Is it better for him to have rooms in college or in lodgings? Is there any preliminary exam? I ask all these questions in reference to Trinity College which I think was yours and Mr. Richards? Has the man to be there any special time? Is there anything which can be paid by friends and not given through the young man himself?"

Mr. Lowndes reassured me about the £200, whereupon, fortified by a certain measure of approval from Bessie, I sought out our solicitor, Mr. Pennington. Mr. Pennington, like our trustee Mr. Phipson Beale, thought my mother totally unbusinesslike, but he had acquired a tepid liking for me. I had discovered that Hilaire and I had a reversionary interest in the Parkes Trust Fund—the fund which produced Bessie's tiny income—and that it would be possible for me to raise a certain amount of money on the reversion so long as Bessie's life interest in that fund was safeguarded. I proposed to Mr. Pennington that he should help me raise £600 and I told him that I wished him to write, once the money was there, to inform Hilaire that "a friend" of the Parkes family was willing to find the money to send him to Oxford for three years.

This was accordingly done and Hilaire's reaction to the proposal is described in the previous chapter. I wrote to my new friend, Frederic Lowndes: "My brother has several friends at Christ Church and we much feared he would want to go there, so I thought Trinity if possible would be a happy medium as to expense. . . . I wish you could see him—he is a good boy and, like you, gets paid for his poetry."

I found not long ago the draft of a letter composed by Frederic Lowndes for Bessie to write to the President of Trinity asking if he would accept Hilaire. My new friend, as I was later to learn during our long and happy married life, had a very short temper. The first time I ever saw it was when I showed him the President's answer, refusing Bessie's request. Bessie then tried the head of another college, who also refused. Perhaps these gentlemen had good reason, for Hilaire had left the Oratory when not quite seventeen, his brief period at the Collège Stanislas had been wasted, and he was still in the French army.

Then a most fortunate event occurred. Bessie met Dr. Jowett, the famous Master of Balliol, at the Westminster Deanery and they had a long talk after which she wrote to him. I remember very well the immense relief with which his answer to her letter filled us. He said it would give him great pleasure to have at Balliol a great-great-grandson of Joseph Priestley. Bessie and I forthwith went to see him, and I wrote to Frederic Lowndes: "We had an interesting time with Dr. Jowett who was specially gracious to me on the duty of a sister to a brother."

As a result of this interview we discovered with dismay that Hilaire would have to pass an examination before being admitted to Balliol, and the name of a certain tutor was recommended to us who consented to take Hilaire into his house while he coached him. Both he and his wife were extraordinarily kind people for, though Hilaire at this time was both unhappy and rebellious, they became very fond of him, and he on his side became devoted to their little children, to one of whom, Evelyn Bell, he subsequently dedicated his *Bad Child's Book of Beasts*.

Up to the last moment, Mr. Bell doubted whether Hilaire would pass the examination, but happily I received the following letter from him: "Your brother passed into Balliol on Thursday, and has since taken rooms in Holywell. He passed practically on his essay which was considered a rather brilliant performance—at least above the average of a good essay; it was about Poetry. His mathematics were not thought very well of and I am not sure if they will encourage him to read the subject. At all events he has made a favourable impression at the start, which is a *great thing*. He leaves us tomorrow, but we shall continue to see him and perhaps I may put a little work in his way; not to interfere with his own, but to steady him a bit. He is in great spirits and will soon, I am sure, be in a whirl of social engagements. A little responsibility on his shoulders would perhaps serve as a weight on the other side of the balance."

Hilaire went up to Oxford at the age of twenty-two. His school contemporary, James Hope, was then in his last year. There cannot have been many undergraduates even of that age who had trained for a while for the French navy, spent a year in the French army, done free-lance journalism in London, travelled steerage across the Atlantic and followed a much loved woman as far as California.

His first success was winning the Brackenbury Scholarship after he had been a short time at Balliol. I heard this piece of news at a party in a house in Portman Square. I found myself being congratulated warmly on Hilaire's success by people who had read of it in that morning's *Times;* I tried not to show too much emotion, but once I was in a hansom I cried with joy all the way home.

Then the *Pall Mall Gazette* for June 12th, 1893, carried the following news item: "The Union on Thursday last discussed Mr. Rankin's motion 'that this House would welcome a European war.' The best speech of the evening was that by Mr. Belloc, the Balliol Demosthenes. Mr. Belloc, who is a French subject, is, by the bye, author of an article on French conscription in this month's *Contemporary*. The war party had it all their own way from a rhetorical point of view, but failed to convince the House, which condemned the motion by a majority of 41." It goes on to say: "On Thursday next Mr. Max Beerbohm Tree has kindly consented to deliver a lecture at the Union debating hall on Imagination."

Hilaire's successes at Oxford did not surprise me for I had a high opinion of his ability, and they brought Bessie the first gleams of real happiness that she had enjoyed since our father's death. As she lived in a world of poetry and imagination, it moves me to see a list of linen and plate she sent to Hilaire. Dated October, 1893 it reads: "3 pairs of sheets, 3 blankets, 3 dusters (pink), 4 tea cloths (blue), 2 glass cloths (red border), 6 teaspoons (Parkes crest), 6 forks (3 crest and 3 P.P.)." I imagine the P.P. stood for her long-dead brother, young Priestley Parkes.

I have sometimes thought that the three years which Hilaire spent at Oxford were the happiest of his life. After he had won the Brackenbury Scholarship, and with the allowance of £200 a year paid to him through Mr. Pennington, he had more money than many of his fellow-undergraduates.

Hilaire had a great admiration for Jowett who believed in his gifts and encouraged him to expect an All Souls' Fellowship, which in fact he never obtained. It is on record that Jowett once said of some famous barrister who had been at Balliol that "he took to poetry and that sort of nonsense"; and that he said of a young man who, it was thought, might be a successor of Tennyson: "If a poet came here, we could never hold him." Yet he was proud of Swinburne and would most certainly have admired Hilaire's later verse. Jowett was an outstanding Oxford personality. He translated Plato and had famous epigrams written about him, of which this is one:

> First come I, my name is Jowett,
> There's no knowledge but I know it.
> I am Master of this College,
> What I don't know is not knowledge.

He died while Hilaire was at Oxford. My brother wrote: "Dearest Mamma. The Master's funeral will take place in a few days. It is a quite irreparable loss—like that of Manning in Catholic England. No one in Oxford had anything approaching his popularity and breadth. The others are all either silly men, or hated by the body of their fellows."

"Balliol, October 30th, 1894. Dearest Mamma. . . . Oxford remains terribly dreary—the climate is probably the most depressing in England. I have called on the Haldanes and the Rhys. And have made the acquaintance of the new Master. He, and especially his old wife, seem to me some of the pleasantest people I have ever met. They are of the old Liberal type—middle-class Scottish cultured, a very useful leaven to Oxford—they are Home Rulers which is interesting to note in connection with the 'Brewer and Atheists' argument of Unionism. If we can once make the opinion in Oxford that Liberalism is even now the superficially 'clever' side, it will have a great effect on the nation, I think, which nation takes its leaders mainly from Oxford and which leaders have hardly any opinions of their own but say what is thought the superficially clever thing. . . . We had a great full-dress debate at the Union on the House of Lords and got up a respectable minority. The reports of it in the papers were not good, but I made a fairly good speech which will bring me nearer the Presidency, though I doubt whether I command a quarter of the votes yet. . . . I am coming to London for ten days to eat Bar dinners in about a week." This last was a new idea but one which gave satisfaction to Bessie.

When Hilaire became President of the Union, the famous debating society of Oxford, Bessie went up to hear him make his inaugural speech. She was told by two different dons that he was the best speaker the Union had had since Gladstone.

Indeed it would be hard to exaggerate the success of Hilaire's Oxford career: it was there that he made his reputation which henceforward suffered no setback. I only regret that I have so few letters belonging to these three important years. On leaving Oxford Hilaire gained a First in History.

On his vacations from Oxford Hilaire usually went to France accompanied by a friend. Once, for instance, Mr. Stead of the *Pall Mall Gazette*—one of the most kind-hearted and intelligent editors who ever existed—suggested to Hilaire that he should "go over to France with a bicycle and a snap camera, spending the next three weeks in bicycling through the most politically important parts of your country. What do you think it would cost, what route do you think you should follow, and what do you think of the scheme? I should require you to get into conversation at each centre where you stopped with the priest, the mayor, the peasants, the schoolmaster and anyone else accessible—of course so far as you could find easy opportunity, and to send me every night what the people you talked to thought of the Elections, what questions interested them."

What I always thought strange was Hilaire's lack of interest in contemporary French literature and his ignorance of the work being done by the French writers of our day. I knew many French writers, but I should be surprised to learn that Hilaire had met any of them. He wrote, as his admirers will remember, essays on the old writers of France; he had a great admiration for Ronsard and delighted in singing his songs.

The literary world of Paris when we were young was strangely divided. Politics, which played so small a part in the English literary world, played a great part in the eyes of French men of letters. There were two crucial issues in France at the time—the first was that France had recovered with such unexpected resilience from the effects of the Franco-Prussian war that it was commonly believed that Germany was tempted to strike again, and periodical German gestures on the international plane reinforced this view. (This was the period before the *Entente Cordiale* with England which, promoted later by the then Prince of Wales—subsequently King Edward VII—was to change completely the political structure of Europe by establishing that alliance between France and England which has dominated Western Europe for fifty years, and put an end to German imperialism.) Most people in England still had a good deal of sympathy with Germany due to such varied motives as a feeling for a common Protestant tradition, and the naïve theories of a common Nordic race which were then being propagated by German professors and finding a response in the way of thinking that we associate in England with the great writer Carlyle. It is worth adding that one of the most consistent critics of the German machine in England, if not the most influential, was Cardinal Newman.

Times have so changed that it is difficult now to realize how challenging it was in English society at that time to exhibit violently pro-French feeling. Opposition may well have accentuated Hilaire's passion for France which was of a fighting kind, as we see in the Oxford Union debate mentioned above and in all his early writings. Yet his attitude was as anomalous with regard to France as it was to England. He was both a Catholic and a Republican at a time before the younger group of French writers such as Charles Péguy had established themselves and created that kind of Catholic Republicanism which is common amongst Frenchmen today. As I have suggested, it is astonishing that he should have had no contact, at least apparently, either with the young men of the Péguy *milieu* or with a conservative writer of the extreme nationalist school who was then at the height of his power, Maurice Barrès. Hilaire's Catholicism precluded of course any contact with a Republican such as Emile Zola who played such a large part in the Dreyfus case.

At the time of Hilaire's undergraduate visits to France, that country was torn asunder by the protagonists and enemies of this French officer of Jewish extraction who was accused by the French army authorities of espionage. All countries in Europe were interested in what was then called *"l'affaire."* My belief, which was also that of Hilaire, was that Dreyfus was guilty. I have known a considerable number of high-ranking French officers in my life, and I could not remember one whom I did not respect and regard as an absolutely honest man. They were all hard-working and honorable. That such men would have condemned a fellow-officer just because he was a Jew I felt to be impossible.

English society, using the word in a narrow sense, was violently pro-Dreyfus, and I remember having a sharp interchange of words at a luncheon party with a distinguished Englishman who became exceedingly angry when I told him the following fact: that I had recently asked a famous French lawyer, who seemed impartial, what he believed to be the truth. He had attended the Rennes trial as a spectator, and he told me that what had made a strong impression on him was the fact, never publicly revealed, that Dreyfus was urgently in need of money for he had already spent a small fortune on a certain woman. This French lawyer was convinced, and I must say he convinced me, that Dreyfus, while not a spy for Germany, had acted as confidential agent for the Russian government. At that time it was of capital importance to the Russians, who had put all their eggs in the French basket, to ascertain the real condition of the French army.

Some years ago I read all the books in the London Library dealing with the Dreyfus Case. In a sense, they made me feel the story to be even more obscure than I had realized. His advocates made him out to be a noble being, without a stain on his character, while the other side regarded him as having been an arch spy. I believe many facts were withheld both by the Dreyfusards and the anti-Dreyfusards. No doubt much was invented and a great deal that was true was never told. The French Government granted Dreyfus a pardon. This enraged his British partisans who felt shocked and disgusted when they learned that Dreyfus eagerly accepted this "pardon." One of them—the late Lord Carlisle—expressed his bitter regret to me that Dreyfus had not thrown it back in their faces.

I know another fact which I think was never published. This was that Sir Charles Russell (later Lord Russell of Killowen) went to Rennes at the request of Queen Victoria to watch the trial. The Queen was a strong Dreyfusard, and she expressed sharp displeasure when Sir Charles Russell reported that Dreyfus had not impressed him favourably. I doubt if any event so divided any country. My French family, who were quite out of the French Jewish world, were strong Dreyfusards, as I believe were most of the French intelligentsia.

In August, 1895, Hilaire went further afield with his friend, Lord Basil Blackwood. "Dearest Mamma. Just a note in the only medium I have to tell you *not to forward anything* either to Haparanda or Gothenburg. We shall make our way down to the sea coast and take ship direct for England. I shall probably be with you on September 3rd or 4th at latest as our boat will probably go to London. We are quite safe and very interested. I will tell you our adventures when I get back. This note is being taken by a trapper going down river to the coast. I hope he posts my letters honestly. He looks honest. He is a Finn and he thinks 1 kroner enormous pay for the job. We have made him understand what we want. Blackwood and I are very dirty, but delighted with the new sights of the north. No game to speak of and interminable forests. I will call at Great College Street and if I land at some other port than London will let you know on landing."

At the beginning of one of his vacations, as is well known, Hilaire walked from Oxford to London setting a record that undergraduates since then have tried in vain to rival. As I have said, his vitality was insatiable.

It was with his friend, Lord Basil Blackwood, that Hilaire wrote *The Bad Child's Book of Beasts,* and since this was published in 1896 it is probable that they discussed it during their 1895 holiday, Hilaire writing the verses and Blackwood doing the illustrations. *The Bad Child's Book of Beasts* was refused by several publishers until finally Hilaire and Blackwood arranged themselves for it to be published. It promptly won a huge success, and for years brought in money for Hilaire.

In spite of Hilaire's dislike of Oxford's climate, he continued to live in that city after going down from the University. He coached private pupils and lectured for the University Extension Lectures and wrote many articles for the reviews. It was during the winter of 1895 to 1896, while pursuing these activities, that he received the dramatic news that brought happiness and a degree of stability into his restless life.

8

EARLY YEARS OF MARRIED LIFE

→»)«←

ALL THROUGH his Oxford career with new friendships with brilliant men and the intensive work that it provided, and with his growing fame, Hilaire never forgot Elodie Hogan. That this was so is proved—if proof were needed—by a little poem scribbled on the back of a letter to Bessie:

> Little Child Jesus was born in a stable;
> I am a child and I pray when I'm able.
> I pray when I'm able—and then at the end
> I remember to pray very hard for a friend
> Who will come in a hollow boat over the sea;
> Little Child Jesus, have mercy on me.

So Bessie's feelings can be imagined when she received the following communication: "Dearest Mamma. I think you ought to know at once—though I have waited a day or two—that Elodie has left the convent and that I am older and better fitted for life by five years. I beg you will tell no one nor act upon it in any way till I have written to one or two people who should know. Notably, Mrs. Charles to whom I shall write today. I shall devote all my energy for the next few days to combining my success in this with the plans for earning my own income. You need not be afraid of my compromising my chances here in any way. I have waited five years and I have done my duty. It almost looks as though I were to be rewarded with a happy life. But I shall not be such a fool as to neglect the opportunities which keep a man and woman with a roof over them and with decent friends. It has brought me back from I cannot tell you what precipices of insanity and despair. . . ."

Almost simultaneously Bessie received news of the death of Mrs. Hogan. Elodie had never been certain of her vocation, and indeed years later Elodie told me that she tried to become a nun chiefly to please her mother.

In a letter to me from Elizabeth Hogan, she enclosed an obituary which reads: "Mrs. Ellen A. Hogan was the widow of the late John S. Hogan, to whom she was married in 1859, her maiden name being Barrett. With her husband she moved to Napa in 1860 and helped him to build up his large business interests. After his death in 1877 she managed the business in a way that would be a credit to any man. Some time ago she took a trip, accompanied by her daughters Elizabeth and Elodie, through Europe, visiting her old home in Ireland. Mrs. Hogan was the possessor of large property interests here, including the Napa Hotel block and other real estate. She was a woman of high character, commanding respect from her acquaintances and love from her family and friends. She leaves six children to mourn her loss: Mrs. Hopkins of the Hawaiian Islands, Misses Elizabeth and Elodie, Henry, Sebastian and John. All were with her at her death. The funeral service was conducted by the Rev. J. Slattery who paid a merited tribute to the late Mrs. Hogan for the noble manner in which she had educated and reared her children that they might become useful members of society."

Hilaire wanted to go straight to California and he obtained enough work in the States through his University Extension Lectures to make this financially possible. Bessie decided to go with him. She had always longed to see America, for not only had she close American friends, but also American relations. My grandmother Parkes had been born at Northumberland, a town on the Susequehanna River.

I had married Frederic Lowndes, who was already a member of the *Times* staff, on January 9th, 1896, at the London Oratory, and my husband and I took over the lease of the Great College Street house. Bessie and Hilaire sailed in March and I soon received Bessie's description of the voyage, written in April, 1896:

"My own darling. I am here, right in the midst of lovely country, and post rather uncertain, so as we are going into the 'City' today I mean to post you a note for the *Britannic*. We had a very good voyage; it is an amazing sensation, being driven in a huge floating *hotel* at the rate of twenty miles an hour for six days and nights. A beautiful iceberg paid its respects to us about five miles off, lying like a huge white cliff on the face of the water. . . . Hilary went to Philadelphia yesterday and came back today for a few hours. He is giving three lectures in Philadelphia and Baltimore and starts for California on Saturday. He behaved *very* kindly to me on the voyage but his mind is unchanged. Gertrude Atherton spoke to him; but he told her he could not care for anyone but Elodie."

In Philadelphia Hilaire earned £20 in one week by lecturing which, as he wrote, "is not too bad."

On May 18th, 1896, having arrived in California, he wrote to Bessie: "Dearest Mamma, this is just a little note to tell you I have got your letter. I was, oddly enough, terribly fatigued with the journey and am just picking up again. Elodie was at death's door while you and I were in New York—they sat up with her ten days and nights. But she is now in *full* convalescence. I have seen her doctor and had a long talk with him—it seems the breakdown was due to that experiment in Maryland—he says she has an excellent constitution and that as she gets well she will be stronger than ever. She takes little walks with me every day, and I go to Mass with Elizabeth."

Hilaire urged Elodie to marry him at once. Elizabeth had married shortly before, and Hilaire's and Elodie's quiet wedding took place from Elizabeth's house on June 15th. They spent a short honeymoon before starting on Hilaire's lecture tour which was immensely successful.

Bessie treasured the first letter he wrote after his marriage: "June 16th, 1896. Dearest Mamma, a word to tell you that you now have a daughter-in-law. We were married yesterday in the early morning and came off here for a little honeymoon of a day or two; she is happy and surprisingly well—I only hope the long journey will not pull her down again. We start on Saturday and should be at Port Kent on the first of next month *for a couple of days,* as I have to be in Philadelphia by the 4th at latest. We remember that it is your birthday and look on that as a good omen—may you continue to have many birthdays. Be good to my wife, my own dearest mother. We have been married in as Catholic a way as could be. With a Nuptial Mass and Communion and all sorts of rites and benedictions by an old priest called Slattery; he stands in great awe of your having met the Archbishop. We also had a great wedding breakfast and you shall have a bit of the cake. She made me go to confession twice before risking the Sacrament, and I will believe what she believes and hold to what she and you hold to. Goodbye. Your affectionate and devoted son."

Towards the end of July Hilaire and Elodie returned to England by slow boat—as "time is no object," he wrote to me.

I remember one day hearing a horse draw up on the cobble-stones in front of the door in Great College Street, and I saw Elodie and Hilaire on the pavement having got out of a hansom cab. They both looked well and happy and were on their way to Oxford where a friend had taken rooms for them in Bath Place.

They stayed a few days in London and I gave Elodie, as my wedding present, a white satin gown. In those days a bride wore a white dress at dinner parties for the first few months after her marriage. Though I myself had been married at the Oratory in a coat and skirt, I was sufficiently conventional to wish that Hilaire's wife should appear, in the critical eyes of the Oxford ladies, in what they would regard as the right kind of evening dress.

In those days we thought Elodie strongly resembled Raphael's lovely portrait of the Fornarina which hangs in the Louvre. As a matter of fact, I think Elodie was far better looking than the Fornarina. She looked much younger and for years retained—even after her children were born—a girlish grace and charm of appearance. In an old book of memoirs called *Adventures of a Novelist,* Hilaire's American friend Gertrude Atherton wrote: "Elodie was a beautiful creature with hair like polished mahogany, eyes of a dark rich blue, regular features, and a mantling colour . . . she also possessed the twin gifts of personality and charm."

The early years of married life were marked by fairly frequent changes of home, the birth of babies, and, on Hilaire's part, desperately hard work to keep his growing family. He went on with his coaching and University Extension Lectures and started writing his own books in earnest. *The Bad Child's Book of Beasts* ("The Beast Book" as it was called in the family), brought in a steady income, as will be seen from his letters. At this time he published at his own expense a slim volume of poetry called *Verses and Sonnets*—a volume now so rare that I have never seen it listed in any second-hand catalogue. Later Elodie advised him to recall the edition as she was convinced that he would be recognized as a poet and would then regret having brought out this early collection of verse. Though there was one good review, this little book was scarcely noticed at all. Yet in my opinion it contains some beautiful work—including the following lines:

> Love wooing Honour, Honour's love did win,
>   And had his pleasure all a summer's day.
> Not understanding how the dooms begin,
>   Love wooing Honour, wooed her life away.
>
> Then wandered he for full five years' unrest,
>   Until, one night, this Honour that had died,
>   Came as he woke, in youth grown glorified,
> And smiling like the saints whom God has blest.
>
> But when he saw her in the clear night shine
> Serene, with more than mortal light upon her,
> The boy that careless was of things divine,
>   Small Love, turned penitent to worship Honour.
> So Love can conquer Honour; when that's past,
>   Dead Honour risen outdoes Love at last.

Hilaire's and Elodie's letters tell the story of the early years of married life:

"November 15th, 1896. 5, Bath Place, Holywell, Oxford. Dearest Mamma. . . . All the young Oxford Liberals who have taken Firsts and been Presidents of the Union are bringing out a book on politics, and I am writing one essay. There are half a dozen. . . . Elodie is looking charming; she has a brown dress just made for her in which she looks so well. Mrs. Cotton was very cordial and we had a delightful visit. Elodie was especially pleased as it was the first time she had seen a *Meet*—a very English sight."

"December 1st, 1896. Dearest Mamma, I was not able to send you a copy of *The Bad Child's Book of Beasts* because the first edition sold out *at once* on my return to Oxford, four days after publication. A second edition is out the day after tomorrow. W. & D. were fools not to take it, as Basil and I have already been paid £20 on advance by the printers for fear we should sell the edition to someone else. I will send you a copy of the first edition (if I can recover it) and in any case two of the second. Here it freezes hard. Elodie unfortunately, unlike me, does not revel in keen cold. There is a question of raising me to Staff Lecturer in the University Extension. That is double my present pay, but it is unlikely, as it would give cause of jealousy to many older men. . . ."

"Sunday, December 13th, 1896. Dearest Mamma. Now the *2nd edition* is all sold in four days again! And we are printing 1,000 more and no limit for the demand. An American edition is to be issued for about £30 *paid up*. Publishers are mere tradesmen, especially in their *limitations*—how different from the old set, John Murray, etc. Elodie is well, better than she has been hitherto. The visit to the Flowers did her a lot of good and she saw the Malvern Hills. Her great delight is to see hills! We start in two days for the States. We spend our last night at Liverpool with Sir John and Lady Brunner. Sir John wants to talk over my essay "The Liberal Tradition" which is appearing in the volume I told you about. I was examined for insuring my life today, and passed as a first-class life, although I told them of my uncle Priestley's early death.

They say my constitution is remarkable. I think they are going to put me on the staff which means either *less travelling and work or more money.*"

And from Elodie at Liverpool on December 22nd, 1896: "Dearest little Mother, tomorrow about noon we sail. We are both very well and both a little tired—with packing and getting ready in general, and Hun from his term's work [Elodie called Hilaire 'Hun'—an abbreviation of Honey-bun, an American term of endearment]. You will be glad and consoled to know that in his examination for his insurance he got a clean bill of health—lungs and heart and all absolutely sound! I have, too, copies of some testimonials he has received apropos of a lectureship which he may get at New College. I know they will please you enormously. I shall send them to you from America as they are now un-get-at-able. I shall write to you at once, if only a line, and perhaps we shall enjoy the luxury of a cable message to Mary if we arrive safe. We both received Holy Communion together this morning. . . . I had hoped to send you a little pair of warm slippers which I had made for you, but I never got further than buying the wool, I have been so busy and away from our nest so much. I saw Mary and Freddie for a minute yesterday. Good-bye and God bless you. Your loving child, Elodie." And Hilaire adds in his neat small writing at the bottom: "I will write when we land and you should get the letter somewhere about or just before the 15th of January. As yet it is calm. . . . 'Beast Book has already made £50—£25 for me."

While in America Elodie was longing to go to California, but very unselfishly gave up all thought of it. She wrote: "My sister Elizabeth has been very ill with pneumonia and is just better of it and I would be an extra responsibility just now. Add to all this Hilary is always happy and quiet when he is with me and I couldn't in the end find it in my heart to leave

him alone with his hard work." Elodie did not like the northern part of the United States. She said "the climate is diaboli-
cal, I would rather be a Californian tree-toad or an Oxford-
shire rook than a millionaire forced to live in Eastern America. . . . California to a Californian is like the 'ould sod' to
an Irishman. The very earth calls to you to come back. Do you
remember the prayer of the old Irish wife dying in a New
York tenement house—'May my soul pass through Ireland
on its way to God'? But I knew it was better to give it up and
Hilary is so good to me that nothing could count with me
where his comfort or welfare are concerned."

"February 23rd, 1897. 1206 Arch Street. My dearest Marie,
we are both well and Hilary's hardest work is over, thank
the Lord! Now we shall have five days together in peace in
Philadelphia. His work has been splendidly successful. I have
an interesting scrap book with cuttings and pictures. Last
week I spent in Germantown with Mrs. Button. They have
all been *so* good to me." Mrs. Priestley Button was Bessie's
cousin who was exceedingly kind to the young couple, as were
all her American friends. While in America, Hilaire and
Elodie were overjoyed at receiving a brilliant review of "The
Beast Book" published in the *Academy*.

Then in March from Hilaire: "Rittenhouse Club, 1811
Walnut Street. Dearest Mamma. . . . Of course you have
seen the Liberal Essays by this time. *I have not* which is rather
base, considering I am the head and font of the thing. I only
hope there will be an attack from the Socialist side. If you
will read *The Isis* for March 20th you will see the first review
by one of the Socialist dons—very bitter though affecting
courtesy. . . . We cross on Saturday on the *Bretagne,* to show
my wife to the friends in Paris, and then we return. We
should be in London *before* the 25th, and then go househunting. I want the country—a *small* house. *Water if possible,*

as sailing is my only amusement. Is it possible to nearly fur-
nish with what we have? I want to show Elodie the Mont St.
Michel and Avranches—later it may be more difficult. . . .
I have the order for a life of Danton from Mallet, £45 down
and royalties—if it is all right it will do for summer work.
Arnold says he will publish any verse I write and is very keen
for the new Child's book, half of which is about written. Basil
is working at the illustrations. I am now £50 to the good on
the last one, and so is he. I hope however it will be paid up
quarterly . . ."

The immediate need for a move from the small rooms in
Bath Place was that Elodie was expecting her first baby. Hilaire wrote to me concerning the cottage he had in mind:
"Elodie and I cannot decide where our cottage is to be, but
it must be in the country. It will be *permanently inhabited*
we hope—if in a cheap place it will be more than a cottage—
I want a *permanent pied-à-terre* which even if I have a professional income of importance should have associations and be a
home for the holidays. These, in every English profession, are
long."

For a time they found rooms—not yet a cottage—in Littlemore, the village near Oxford where Newman lived during
his last period as an Anglican. Elodie wrote in 1897 to Bessie:
"The Grange, Littlemore, Oxon. Dearest little Mother. . . .
We are most comfortably fixed here. We have two rooms, a
great big bedroom with a huge wide bed and a nice little
sitting-room opening through glass doors on to a beautiful
old garden and orchard. I feel as if I were millions of miles
from Oxford and yet Hilary runs in on his wheel in 15 minutes! He has gone to work again on his *Political Germany*,
and works on his English syllabi. The food is very good as
we order it ourselves and we try to avoid what they do badly.
Hilary has left off wine and takes beer, which perhaps helps

to make him sleep. If I had known of this place I would have brought you up here to see Cardinal Newman's little Anglican Monastery. Since I lived in Rome among the relics of the Saints of God I know of nothing that has touched me more than the ugly narrow one-storied row of rooms opening upon a bare and ugly lane where those wonderul men lived together and faced the Light that showed God's truth. They had no cloistered peace nor trees nor grass nor groined roof nor mullioned windows; a little bare square room for solitude and one larger room for food, I suppose, and common room. Cardinal Newman built the church here while he was vicar. His mother, Jemima Newman, laid the cornerstone in 1835. In 1836 she died, before its completion. There is a touching tablet on the north wall of the church recording these facts. The Cardinal lived in the Monastery from the summer of '43 until his baptism on October 5th, 1845, and then stayed on until the summer of 1846. The following is a copy of a letter to some friends dated Jan. 20, 1846: 'You may think how lonely I am. *Obliviscere populum tuum et domum patris tui* has been in my ears for the last twelve hours. I realize more, that we are leaving Littlemore and it is like going on the open sea.' He is still remembered by many old people in the village and always with the most tender respect and love. One old cottage woman has sent me in a great pile of photographs and prints of him and a book of his sermons. It is very wonderful to walk along the lane from the church to the monastery and to know he went backwards and forwards following his duty. What a heritage he has left England!"

As I reread Elodie's letters I am struck by her good sense and courage. This one belongs to the same period: "*Danton* will soon be published now. Also *The Modern Traveller* and *The City of Paris*. I am glad to say that Hilary is very well. He sleeps well and works hard at a new list of historical research. It was a serious business for us to give up the University Extension Lectures, but I am convinced it was a good thing to do—as he was so utterly gone to pieces when he got home from America."

Hilaire's capacity for work, as may be seen, was prodigious. But he was able now and then to take a holiday. When he could not sail, he walked. "Porbridge-on-Tyne, June 24th, 1897. Dearest Mamma, I would have written for your birthday and was intending to. But the hurry of the last week at Oxford was fearful. Elodie is staying with Mrs. Smith, the wife of my tutor, and I am off walking north. I have never been north before, it is a fine country but spoilt in every way by the commercial necessities of England. Durham is especially fine, the finest group of buildings I have seen in England. But all around it are collieries and dirt. The town is spoilt by them. From here I get into more open country, right into the Cheviot Hills. Today I saw the mountain of Cheviot forty or fifty miles off from a high bridge. They have a fine way here of building villages on the tops of hills. Since Durham I have been following the old British and Roman road. In most places a modern road runs along it. I have taken many sketches and hope to take many more before I get to Edinburgh."

Elodie wrote: "I think you will be glad to know that before the summer is over we are going to have a cottage—a home somewhere—wherever it will be best all round. It will be permanent and a home indeed. . . ." But this wish was not realized, for the autumn saw the young Bellocs back in the heart of Oxford, at No. 36 Holywell, one of the smallest townhouses I have ever seen. It was here that their first child was born. To Bessie's great pleasure he was named Louis after our father.

On October 4th, 1897, Hilaire wrote to Bessie: "Dearest

Mamma, Elodie is progressing admirably up to now. So is the boy. I hope you will bless me with your hands and forgive my failing in duty to yourself, as thus the boy will have a greater chance of turning out well. He is, they tell me, exceptionally healthy and he is to be baptized a fortnight hence. That is, three weeks after his birth. I have asked John Phillimore and John Norris to be Godfathers. Mrs. Biddulph will be Godmother. I have delightful letters from everyone; some fifty in all which will take a long time to answer. I will put you up any time you want to see him. I am very tired, but I am to have £25 for what is comparatively easy work."

Hilaire was a good and loving father and Elodie an excellent mother. I should like to put on record here something of her tenderness and sweetness. Perhaps Louis lay particularly close to her heart: certainly she never wrote a letter without mentioning him.

"Come here whenever you can," she wrote to Bessie. "The Boy is the dearest thing in the universe. He is amiable and sweet and quiet and sleeps well and we hardly know he is here until food time comes! Then a cry comes from Israel! I am sure he grows every hour and is *so* well, by God's grace."

"The Beast Book" was still proving an invaluable standby financially. "It is selling like wild fire—150 have sold in two days," wrote Hilaire, "and more must have sold during the course of yesterday for the publishers are sending to me to arrange for yet another reprint. I am delighted at this as it means a profit of £5 on every hundred sold after the 350 is passed. . . . Urquhart has been elected a fellow of Balliol. There are ten Oratory boys undergraduates up here now. Isn't that a good thing!" This undated letter must have been written, I believe at Christmas time, to explain the fresh sales of "The Beast Book."

During the University vacations Hilaire usually went off on long tramps and he often went abroad, sometimes with a man friend. Elodie's letters were more frequent when he was away.

"March 18th, 1898. 36 Holywell. Dearest Grandmamma [as she called Bessie from the time of Louis's birth], Mary is coming down for a day and night by herself some time next week. I had a cheerful nice long letter from Hun yesterday. Won't we be glad to see each other again! I dream of him at night. Louis is lovely, God bless him! He is going out in a few minutes. I dined with Miss Peto the night before last when I met Monsignor Nugent. He is a wonderful old man of nearly 80. He knew all our old clerical friends in California. It was like a breath of home to meet him."

"March 28th, 1898. 36 Holywell. Dearest Grandmamma, we finished our blessed little retreat yesterday morning. It has done us a world of good—even bodily for I had to be up at 7 every morning so I had to go to bed before 10 every night. Oxford has been as cold as the North Pole. Louis has not been out for a week. But he is so lovely! He slept 8 hours straight last night without a move! . . . Up in our little print-shop there has been for some days a most lovely picture of your old friend Dr. Samuel Parr. Also a splendid one of Napoleon. What lessons in history and biography you could give me from that window!"

In the summer of 1898 Hilaire's love of sailing took him to Hemingfleet near Lowestoft. "Dearest Mamma, Elodie and I are going off for my birthday to Wroxham where there is a regatta. Phillimore has been with us for a few days and found this place lovely. Would you care to come here for a while? You must let us know, if so, what date will suit you and we will arrange it easily. It is three hours from London. Do not consider the expense. Elodie sends her love. Louis has no tooth yet! But he is enormous. He also seems extremely healthy and tries very hard to talk. He cannot, it seems, shape any words until he has teeth, but he has all the tone; he laughs a great deal. If I were you I would come up. It is a lovely old house with a 'walled garden.' "

Elodie had all the Irish woman's violence of feeling over any political question, and when Bismarck died in 1898 she wrote: "I have been horrified at the press on Bismarck. Since Genghis Khan and Tamerlane he was the worst man that trod this unhappy earth for its sins, and centuries of suffering will come from his vile ideas. A bandit without chivalry or courtesy—a glutton, an atheist, everything revolting to all the highest and best part of mankind. And yet we hear *ad nauseam* about the strong man, etc., etc. And only one weak little Royalist sheet in Paris has dared to call him names—'the old malefactor' was their dignified and just way of calling him. Hilary told me Tuesday morning of his death. . . . . . . How different from Mr. Gladstone! The one conscious of Death's approach, mild, praying, believing in and looking towards Almighty God; he dies with all his works gone to ashes —nothing stable, nothing sure, nothing done. Bismarck smokes his pipe, complains that he can't have more spirits in his water, is suddenly clutched by the agony of Death and dies, seeing his evil works built upon lying, lack of principle, materialism, cynicism, flourishing and strong. Sad world is this we live in! God keep and preserve our Holy Father Leo XIII, for he is now the only man except the Emperor Francis Joseph who has any hold upon the safe things for human affairs. I suppose his days are really numbered now, but God may lengthen them."

The letter ends on a domestic note: "Louis is most lovely to look upon. Also wise and amiable and very healthy. His teeth show no signs of being nearer. I suppose they will burst upon an astonished household suddenly some night. He has pulled himself up so miraculously that I daresay it has used his 'tooth-energy' as the Germans would put it."

The *Life of Danton* was finished by now, and Hilaire had embarked on a book about Robespierre "He has begun a book on Robespierre to come out in the spring (D.V.)," wrote Elodie. "He and Lord Basil are at work on another Christmas book—a rhyming nonsense alphabet. I think it is very funny. Then there is a new *History of Paris* for Arnold." This book was also published by Coates of Philadelphia, and Hilaire got £50 advance.

He found writing his historical books a great strain. "Dearest Mamma, I did not write before this because I was so immersed in work that one day went by after another without my knowing quite how they passed. I am writing *Robespierre* as fast as possible. I spent 14 hours at it one day and have spent 8 today. It is the only way of writing history, to accumulate first a full impression and then to write at top speed, but it is a noble labour."

Hilaire and Elodie sometimes visited London in the vacations. When they did this they stayed in lodgings near Great College Street. This letter to Bessie, who was living in Slindon, belongs, I think, to Christmas 1898: "Elodie and I went to Midnight Mass and to Communion. The Oratory was full up to the corners—half Protestants and half Catholics. There were 800 people at Communion. I have not seen so many since I was in Paris last Christmas Eve."

Although Hilaire had given up his lecturing, he had not yet given up coaching private pupils, as the following letter from Elodie shows: "June 22nd, 1899. . . . You know what Oxford is in term time, and although I am entirely withdrawn from everything, still even so one is caught in the maelstrom more or less. Besides this we have been making all Louis's summer clothes at home and I have been kept busy making button-holes, besides arranging for the little stranger's coming. I have a very good servant, and nurse has been as good as she can be of late. Hilary is very well. He has altogether 14 men in the final school—some five or six of these he had coached entirely so it was a busy and anxious time for us. We are keenly looking out for the lists."

The "little stranger" was a daughter born on July 14th, 1899, and baptized Eleanor. Bessie had Louis to stay with her during this time, and when he and his nurse returned to Holywell, Elodie wrote: "August 14th, 1899. Dearest Grandmamma, the travellers arrived safe and tired about 2 o'clock yesterday. Louis wept at first when he was introduced to Eleanor but in a few minutes he loved her and was much appeased when she loved his hand where a wasp had stung him. She is getting on splendidly in spite of the dreadful weather and has gained nearly 2 lbs. since her birth. She is very sweet and looks like Louis when he was a mite. I must thank you a thousand times for all your care of Louis and Nurse. As a thank offering for baby's safe arrival we are giving Nazareth House bread, beans and potatoes! Both children are thus their benefactors and are prayed for every day."

Like all home-makers, Elodie made much of feastdays and festivals. She wrote on December 18th, 1899: "I am going to give dear little Louis a real Christmas. I am getting a tree for him and for a few other little ones on Sunday; then on Christmas Day I shall light the tree up again for six or seven of the tiny Nazareth House babies."

Then, quite suddenly, Hilaire decided to leave Oxford, which had been his home now for eight years, and move to London. This decision did not, however, mean that he intended to give up tutoring and devote himself entirely to writing, for he still coached private pupils in his London home in the midst of his writing and journalism. In fact the amount of work he got through was amazing. Perhaps his decision to move to London was partly influenced by the fact that he cherished hopes of being called to the Bar (for which, it will be remembered, he had eaten his dinners as an undergraduate). But in fact—which seemed to Bessie and me astounding—he was actually "ploughed" for the Bar examination. Had he passed, his whole after life would have been different.

9

"MY LITTLE HOUSE IN CHEYNE WALK"

※≫≫≪≪

THE HOUSE Hilaire and Elodie chose in London was in
Cheyne Walk, Chelsea. It was well-built, at least twice as large
as our house in Great College Street, and had beautiful views
of the Thames, which was probably why Hilaire chose it, as he
loved overlooking water. I naturally regretted that they had
not chosen a home in Westminster, for leases of charming
houses could be obtained for small sums in the streets near
Great College Street, and Chelsea seemed a long way from
Westminster in those days. Those who know Hilaire's verse
will recall a very funny rhyming letter to E. V. Lucas in which
he gives, in my opinion, a fanciful picture of 36 Cheyne Walk.
I quote two lines:

> A little aged cracked neglected house
> And painted white in front
> But Home to me.

The nursery in the Chelsea house was large and airy, and it
was there that Hilaire's third child, Elizabeth, was born.

At the time of the move Bessie had not been well and
Hilaire was worried: "Do, my darling mother, reply to me

about your health and believe in my devotion to you. Elodie sends you her love." There follows news of the children: "Eleanor cannot *yet* talk but understands everything and is delightful. Louis said yesterday '*I am a loving brother*' with great unction to distinguish himself from Eleanor who had just put her finger down the baby's throat. Eleanor pulled his hair violently from rage knowing that he was blaming her by implication. Elizabeth grows in grace and can smile. . . . I write, lecture and teach every hour of my waking moments. *Robespierre* is in sight of the end. God bless you."

Very soon after the move to London, Elodie had the one great sorrow of her life. This was the death of her sister Elizabeth, who was expecting her first child. The two sisters had been devoted to one another and Elizabeth's death was a fearful blow to Elodie. She wrote to Bessie: "For twenty years and more Elizabeth and I have been close friends—so near to each other. We always understood everything. I feel as if I had been suddenly deprived of one of the powers of my soul. It has made me ill and miserable. I take refuge in constant prayers for her for I know she is somewhere watching and knowing. That strong heroic soul that left her body in doing her duty has not gone out. What a blessing it is to be even the worst and humblest child of the Church."

Troubles never come singly and soon after the move to the new house the following exasperating incident occurred, recounted by me in a letter to Bessie: "I am writing to tell you of an annoying occurrence which happened yesterday at Chelsea. Elodie's nursemaid let fall a lamp and set fire to the two nurseries. Fortunately she and the nurse, helped by the cook, got the children out. Everything in the two rooms was burnt, in fact they are completely destroyed, but Hilaire and some men he got in from the street kept the fire down till the engines arrived. It might have been so much worse that I think

Elodie can only feel thankfulness today. All the children's clothes have been burnt, but nothing of any real value. The salvage men were there all night preventing the fire from breaking out again. They are properly insured. Elodie wished me to tell you as she feared you might hear of it and get startled. I am going down to see them this afternoon and will either telephone to you or write a line this evening. I have learnt all this through the telephone this morning. The nurse seems to have saved the children's lives by her energy and sense. The baby's cot was already in flames when she snatched the child out."

But the worst misfortune of all during the London period was the one serious illness of Hilaire's early life.

He had been over-working terribly, as will presently be seen. He had to make the journey from Chelsea to Fleet Street —about four miles—every day, which was fatiguing on top of his arduous "pot-boiling." He was constantly preoccupied about money to keep his growing family and to meet the cost of living in London—I recall his telling me that they were spending three times as much money in London as they had spent in Oxford. Elodie liked the house to be well staffed and for most of the London period they had two servants in addition to the children's nurse. The rent of the house was low, but they were fond of entertaining and frequently had friends to dinner, for they had around them an amusing set of people of their own age and interests. In 1902 a fourth child was born, a son, Hilary; and in 1904 the fifth and last, Peter.

Perhaps Hilaire's sudden, severe attack of influenza was not surprising. Pneumonia set in. A trained nurse Elodie had known in Oxford was sent for, but could not come. I recall every moment of that terrible winter day when Elodie telephoned and told me that she thought Hilaire was dying. I obtained a trained nurse through my own doctor and took her to Chelsea in a four-wheeler. The day was foggy and it became so thick at the corner of Cheyne Walk that the cabman refused to go any further, and the nurse and I dragged her trunk along the pavement till we got to number 36. In the hall stood the family doctor, an Irishman. He met me at the door and said how sad to think that such a fine young man should be dying, leaving a wife and so many little children. I told him that if he would undertake to get a specialist I would pay the fee; and after what seemed to be hours the specialist arrived. Hilaire was anointed that night. I believe it was the young nurse I had brought with me who finally pulled him through this illness—her constant care coupled with his exceptionally good constitution.

Hilaire's devoted circle of friends sent help of every kind. I remember seeing long cylinders being brought into the house and being told that they contained oxygen. When Hilaire took a turn for the better he became convalescent surprisingly quickly, and Lord Stanley of Alderley lent him his house in Penrhos, Wales, in which to recuperate. After some weeks he was as strong as he had ever been.

Though Bessie was not given to talking to either of us about our literary work nor interfering in our lives in any way, she did speak to Hilaire after his illness and made a strong appeal that he should give up journalism. She told him—for, as is not unusual, she was cleverer when dealing with other people's affairs than with her own—that he was throwing away his remarkable literary gifts and that writing original work would in the long run be of far greater advantage to him than the kind of hard work in which he was engaged. Needless to say he did not take her advice.

Apart from these setbacks, I believe the first six years of this century were as tranquil as any in Hilaire's life.

The amount of writing he did at this time can only be described as prodigious. He never refused a commission. His knowledge of business was small, his need of money urgent. To the best of my belief he never tried to drive any kind of bargain, and when many years later there was a question of a collected edition of his work, it proved impossible to achieve, so many were the publishers who owned his copyrights.

Journalism, being topical, is naturally governed by the writer's attitude to the questions of the day. At the beginning of the century the burning question was the Boer War. Like my husband and myself, Hilaire was pro-Boer. "Dearest Mamma," he wrote in March, 1901, "politics are very stagnant and no one in the know has the least idea of the War being over before 1902—I think it will end in a compromise. Meanwhile Consols are down to 95 which is a drop of twenty in two years! I am awfully afraid that when the Budget is declared (April 18th) they may drop to 90 and affect all securities. The Government will not get out of this War without adding at least £100,000,000 to the national debt, and I doubt if we shall see the Income Tax at less than a shilling again.

"The Opposition has gone utterly to pieces and the only sign of any future value in politics is a small Radical Party that may easily grow into a true disciplined force as the old Corn Law Repeal did. But there now exists a force which did not exist then, the cosmopolitan financier and his newspapers. On the matter of this War, for instance, they prevent the ordinary public getting any news, and it is only if one gets letters from private friends, and meets them at home that we see the desperate hole we are in. Chamberlain's health has quite given way. If he were not the kind of regular man he is, I should say he was taking drugs. Three quarters of the activity of the House is occupied by the Irish—I think they will get Home Rule at any time; it is deplorable that what was refused as a just measure should come now from a sense of weakness."

And: "*The Speaker* is now paying me extra money; the great change in feeling with regard to the War has got me steady *literary* work on *The Pilot;* and especially well-paid work, not night work, on *The Daily News,* where so far the new people think a lot of me. First and last, I see little doubt that, with everything settled, the tide has turned; though I superstitiously touch wood as I write that sentence. . . . To-day I lunched with Sauer who is one of the most interesting men I have met for a long time, and who has just seen Chamberlain with the object of trying to get terms for South Africa. He had a very poor opinion of Chamberlain's abilities."

A couple of years later Hilaire was made literary editor of *The Morning Post* with which he had been linked in lesser capacities for some time. The salary was, I think, £500 a year and it was the first time he had earned a regular income of any size. While on *The Morning Post* Hilaire persuaded Bessie to contribute a paper on Mrs. Gaskell whom she had known in her youth. The article was not signed, but it brought many letters of appreciation from admirer's of Mrs. Gaskell and a touching letter—which gave Bessie great pleasure—from Mrs. Gaskell's only surviving daughter. It was also in *The Morning Post* that Bessie wrote an account of a visit she paid to Haworth with Mrs. Gaskell not long after Charlotte Brontë's death.

And now for Hilaire's books written in this incredibly fruitful period. By far the most famous is *The Path to Rome*. I possess a prospectus of this book giving a specimen page and a drawing of the young Moselle near its source. The book is announced for April 10th, 1902. In his introduction Hilaire wrote the following account of how it came to be written:

"If you should ask how this book came to be written, it was in this way. One day as I was wandering over the world I came upon the valley where I was born, and stopping there a moment to speak with them all—when I had argued politics with the grocer, and played the great lord with the notary-public, and had all but made the carpenter a Christian by force of rhetoric—what should I note (after so many years) but the old tumble-down and gaping church that I love more than mother-church herself, all scraped, white, rebuilt, noble and new, as though it had been finished yesterday. I entered and there saw that all within was as new, accurate and excellent as the outer part; and this pleased me as much as though a fortune had been left to us all; for one's native place is the shell of one's soul, and one's church is the kernel of that nut.

"Moreover, saying my prayers there, I noticed behind the high altar a statue of Our Lady, so extraordinary and so different from all I had ever seen before, so much the spirit of my valley, that I was quite taken out of myself and vowed a vow to go to Rome on pilgrimage and see all Europe which the Christian Faith has saved; and I said, 'I will start from the place where I served in arms for my sins; I will walk all the way and take advantage of no wheeled thing; I will sleep rough and cover thirty miles a day, and I will hear Mass every morning; and I will be present at High Mass in St. Peter's on the Feast of St. Peter and St. Paul. . . .' "

Bessie expressed some concern when Hilaire told her of his project, but he wrote to reassure her: "I would not be afraid about the heat if I were you, for I shall walk in the early mornings and evenings, and rest in the middle of the day. Moreover I am assured that the heat does not really begin in Lombardy till they are fairly into June. The Riviera is, of course, a great deal hotter, but I shall not touch it, as the whole road is either in the Alps or the Apennines; I shall not run the risk even of any specially hot weather save on the little stretch between Como and Piacenza which are in the plains."

The letter goes on: "I am very glad I have got this book ordered, and so eagerly jumped at. It will be the first work I have ever done in my life which I shall be able to write naturally. Everything else has either been history, which is a terrible strain, worse I suppose than any other kind of writing and usually not undertaken save by men of leisure, or else verse which requires very strict care in every part of it and is often very difficult to continue after a certain point. In this book I shall write just what I feel inclined as I go along, and I shall illustrate it with a lot of my own sketches which will be a great joy to me. It will be the only real holiday longer than four days I have had for years, though I often get little scraps of leisure in the intervals of my work."

While Hilaire was on his way Elodie wrote to Bessie: "I had a long letter this morning from Hun, written from Brienz on Friday. To use his own words—'More than a third of the way to Rome—my heart gay and my foot light.'"

That Hilaire was sent far and wide by publishers to collect material for books is shown in a much later letter: "The other day I went over to Bayeux, carefully looking at the Tapestry, on which I am going to write an account for Chatto and Windus, which work is very well paid. I walked also to Honfleur of which I have lively memories from my childhood. The beautiful little chapel on the top of the hill has become a very famous place of pilgrimage. I have the opportunity for a real holiday when this affair is over and I shall be happy to take it for I have not had a real holiday for a very long time. My expedition to Russia, for instance, was not a holiday; it was continual travelling and overshadowed by the fact that I was doing it for a book; and this has nearly always been the case in the last few years—I mean whenever I have got away it has been in connection with some kind of work that has been ordered. This time I shall put the very thought of work right out of my mind. I have a great deal ahead of me because I am writing a continuation of Lingard's *History,* and a *History of France* as well. . . .

And in 1904: *"Emanuel Burden* was splendidly reviewed and is just going into its second edition. I have also brought out another book called *The Old Road* which is a good enough piece of work, but the publishers have brought it out as an edition de luxe and charge a guinea and a half for it. So it will not have a very wide circulation. The work is very much more than last year, but oddly enough is not tiring me so much."

In the year before the War he published no less than five books. One, *The River of London,* was much admired by Bessie. Hilaire had an extraordinary knowledge of London, dating from his childhood, and he owed a great deal of it to our mother. His output was the more remarkable in that he had no regular secretary at this time and wrote all his books by hand—in his extremely small handwriting modelled, I sometimes think, on Cardinal Newman's. His ceaseless output undoubtedly did his reputation harm at the time, though no book shows any sign of having been a mere "pot-boiler." I recall seeing the notes for his *Marie Antoinette*—they filled a trunk! Moreover he was among the first writers on historical events who took enormous trouble in making himself acquainted with the actual places where the battles he described had taken place. He had been fascinated, it might be said from childhood, by the art of war, and long before the outbreak of the First World War, he had visited and walked over all the great battlefields of Europe. It is a curious fact that he never wrote on one subject that he had made completely his own—that of the Moors in Spain.

His writing while in London did not preclude tutoring. "I do a certain amount of coaching," he wrote to Bessie. "Lord

Berwick comes to me next week for this, and I take one of the Herberts." Nor did it preclude his putting in for other jobs —whose exact nature I cannot remember: "The Glasgow chances, I hear, are less than they were, as Balliol is running a candidate—a certain Barker. No one knows him, and no one ever will, but several people have since told me that Religion is insuperable. One must be Protestant, Atheist or Jew—it is a rule."

The "scraps of holiday" he refers to in his letters were of this kind: "The children are well enough. I go sailing for three days tomorrow or next day which I find a great boon, as no letters or papers can reach me."

Elodie writes: "Hun and I spent a happy day at Kew—it was like heaven. Louis ran and jumped and shouted and laughed for hours. I never saw such joy, like a disembodied spirit whose course has just begun."

Once a more ambitious holiday was planned—that of taking the children and the nurse to France. And owing to the wonderful kindness of Barbara Bodichon's sister-in-law, Charlotte Leigh-Smith, who took children and nurse into her home in Brittany, Hilaire and Elodie were able to go off on their own.

"Beauvais, March 22nd, 1904. The day is heavenly. We went twenty miles this morning through the most delightful country, getting here for lunch. We go on to Chantilly. Do you know Beauvais? The Cathedral gives the greatest impression of height of any building in the world. Only the choir was never finished. . . . It is as a fact the highest nave in Europe. I hope you will be in London when we come back in ten days or so. Elodie enjoys this very much. She has had few holidays. Always your affectionate son, H. Belloc."

Hilaire and Elodie went, as often as they could, to stay with

Hilaire's devoted friend George Wyndham and his wife, Lady Grosvenor, at Saighton Grange, near Chester. Elodie wrote to Bessie on one of these occasions: "I thought it might amuse you to hear of our delightful visit here with Lady Grosvenor and Mr. Wyndham. Lady Grosvenor is one of the nicest, best and kindest women whom I have ever met. She has the remains of great beauty but is, I should think, neither strong nor well. But I have never seen greater sweetness of mien. She and Mr. Wyndham have one son, Percy—about 19. He, too, is both beautiful and enlightened. The house is small, but with lovely gardens and an old 13th century tower with a lovely medieval statue of Our Lady. Our Lord, who is in her arms, has had His head taken off by the Cromwellians, I suppose."

Elodie was clever, well-read and an excellent talker. In the busy social life which she and Hilaire enjoyed, she always made her mark. "Last night I met John Murray at dinner. He told me his grandfather had a long and splendid correspondence with *grandmère* Swanton Belloc. She sent him the pair of pistols which Sir John Moore had on his person when he was killed in battle. They were brought to Hilary's French grandfather by a soldier, and when she came in touch with John Murray our grandmother asked him to send the pistols to the sisters of Sir John Moore, and they left them in due course to Mr. Murray."

Again: "Last night we met Lord Halifax at dinner. He was most interesting and devoted himself to me nearly all the evening. I found him mild, charitable, Christian and sincere. He says we all must have 'great patience and great energy.' He talked a lot about Oxford. He adores the memory of Cardinal Manning." She moves on to domesticities: "On Friday a nice elderly cook comes in—for a month on trial! I have not great hopes of her staying, but it will give me time to look about me. . . . Marie and Hilary are dining together at the Author's Club tonight. Eleanor, whom God may bless, is like a rose."

At this time Hilaire owed much kindness to John Buchan, who had already distinguished himself as one of Lord Milner's "young men," and many of his friends believed he would become one of the great pro-consuls who played so considerable a part in the English history of the nineteenth century. He was evidently drawn to a political career, but went first into the publishing house of John Nelson, in Edinburgh. I believe he was among those friends who urged Hilaire into politics. He died as Governor-General of Canada.

Ever since Hilaire had left Oxford, a group of his friends had been trying to persuade him to stand for Parliament in the Liberal interest. One reason for his not doing so was that he would have to give up his French nationality. However, he finally made up his mind to be naturalized as an Englishman, and he wrote to Bessie triumphantly in May 1904: "Dearest Mamma, I do not know whether you have seen in the papers that I have at last got a constituency. It is a division of Manchester, and it is called South Salford. I am extremely glad, for I was getting tired of never being adopted on account of my religion."

He and Elodie went north together for the campaign before the next Election which fell in 1906. Elodie kept Bessie posted with the news: "Alderley Park, Chelford, Crewe. January 3rd, 1906. Dearest Grandmamma, ever since I have been in the North I have intended writing you and giving you a report of things. But somehow the days go by like a flash. We have a stiff fight to make—but I keep my hopes up. My efforts are confined to calling upon and pleasing the women folk of the rich middle-class men who are working for and supporting Hun. The voters are almost entirely of the working class and so I have only shown myself to them at one meeting. When the Chairman told them who I was they all (500) stood up and clapped and cheered and waved their hats. It was very jolly but I nearly died of shyness. I was moved to tears to look at their poor faces—so sober, so tired and so sad. But they were delighted with Hun. They all smoked, he with them. It was an organized 'heckling' meeting for Hun merely to answer questions. Finally they roared for a speech which he gave them. The upshot of it was that he was officially and unanimously declared the candidate for the Socialists and workmen. I have not gone again on the platform as I am sure they feel constrained with a woman of our class in their presence. They like to know that I am about, but they also like noise and fun and fuss at the meetings. However, on Monday we are to have a great meeting in the Town Hall with women, police, etc., etc. I am going then. Do like an angel promise some Masses for the Souls in Purgatory if Hun gets in. It will make a great difference to our fortunes and the future of the children.

"I have found all the women quite delightful. They have virtues that in union with the Sacraments would make this world a Heaven. Lady Stanley has made me make this house my headquarters. I cannot tell you how good she is. Only the family is here and it is quite delightful. I have never seen a happier family in my life. . . . It is only now that I realize how utterly worn out I have been. I have never really got over the shock and terror of Hilary's illness. I still wake every night from 2 to 4 o'clock in the morning. It was then that I used to go down to see him."

An interesting offshoot of Hilaire's election campaign was a letter he received from old Mr. Phipson Beale, Bessie's trustee—who, having heard him address a large meeting in Manchester, sent him his cordial congratulations and said: "It will be pleasant to live to see a grandson of Joe Parkes enter the House. I regret to say that I am one of the few survivors at the Reform Club who knew him well."

It is a curious fact that Hilaire thought the chances were against him and was surprised when he was returned. He certainly made a great impression in the constituency.

His election to Parliament caused Bessie intense pleasure. She, too, thought back to her father, "Joe" Parkes, who had played a considerable part behind the political scenes of his day, especially in the passing of the Reform Bill in 1833. Indeed one of her earliest recollections was of having stood, as a child of four, at the door of her parents' house in Great George Street to see her father start in a postchaise to give Birmingham the first news of the passing of the Bill. To the very end of her life, and she died at the age of ninety-four, she remained absorbedly interested in politics, and especially in all that went on in the House of Commons.

My husband and I spent most of that Election night on the Embankment in London seeing the returns come in. I remember the exultation and excitement I felt when I saw Hilaire's name appear on the huge placards outside the National Liberal Club, on which the returns were flashed.

In spite of his remarkable gift for public speaking, Hilaire did not often speak in the House of Commons. When he did he made a mark. The substance of one of his speeches was greeted on both sides of the House with good-humoured incredulity. In the course of it he advocated a vast increase in the artillery of the British army and made it clear that he believed that Germany would some day attack Britain. I remember one of his circle of devoted friends saying that it was a great pity that Hilaire had this "bee in his bonnet," as though the German Emperor was always rattling his sword, but was really a timorous man and would never go to war.

While in Parliament Hilaire wrote a play called *Behind the*

Speaker's Chair. But when, during the 1914 to 1918 War, an American producer proposed to put it on, Hilaire refused, as he did not think it suitable that anything which cast ridicule on the House of Commons should be put on during a war.

I would like to make two comments while dealing with this phase of Hilaire's life: one, that one of his many idiosyncracies was that of having a great dislike of women taking part in public life. This was the more surprising when it is remembered that his mother, whom he admired enormously, had spent many years of her youth working for what were then called "Women's Rights." My second comment concerns Hilaire's political life in general. After standing for Parliament in 1906 as a Liberal, he stood on another occasion as an Independent and again he was returned. My husband, who had a great knowledge of English political life, always maintained that had he not stood as an Independent he might have had a remarkable political career, so great was his gift of public speaking and so remarkable his personal power over those who felt themselves to be in sympathy with even some of his views.

10

KING'S LAND

After five years of life in London the young Bellocs found that the strain and expense were too great. Elodie and her husband started househunting in the country, and she asked Bessie to tell her of any house she heard of, so it was not surprising when they finally moved to Slindon to a house called Courthill.

In March 1905 Elodie wrote to Bessie: "Blessed be the Lord! Your letter was good news. Last night it was ratified by a great bunch of wall-papers coming for us to choose from. After my life here in Chelsea I feel as if a new era was beginning. Since we must leave this lovely spot I am glad of the complete break and I shall not be surprised if we settle down into Courthill as a permanency—but that is for the future to decide. In any case it will be a great blessing to be near Mass. I must say that my courage quakes at the prospect of the move. But I daresay I shall pull through it as I have pulled through other things. I am not well—I seem to have consumed all my interior reserve of energy and good spirits. Peter the beloved was short-coated on Saturday in honour of the Annunciation."

As it turned out, however, they did not stay in Courthill for long, but it was their home when Hilaire was first in Parliament. The children were so happy to be in the country, and I for my part was delighted that the young Bellocs had chosen a house near Bessie's as this meant that my three children, who frequently stayed with their grandmother—as we had no country home at that time—were able to be with their cousins constantly and form warm ties of affection, which have endured into grown-up life.

There were some happy letters from Courthill. "August 26th, 1906. Dearest Grannie, many thanks for your offer of the sofa—I really have no place to put it, and upstairs I have two or three nice little beds upon which I can rest. It is the effort to get away from the household that I fail in. Hun arrived safe and happy on Thursday evening. He is now riding the mare up on the downs with a delightful Irishman who was with him in the Pyrenees. He returns to London for his Oxford lecture tomorrow. He will be sure to look you up." Bessie was paying one of her constant visits to me in Westminster at the time. My husband and I had moved to 9 Barton Street, a beautiful little house close to Great College Street, which was our beloved home for nearly thirty years.

Hilaire and Elodie did not care enough for Courthill to make an offer to buy it. From there they continued to search for a house they loved enough to make their permanent home. Altogether they considered eighty houses—Hilaire riding a large bicycle and pulling Elodie in a trailer made of wicker.

One day they had an order to view an old farm house near the village of Shipley, some miles from Horsham. As they rounded the bend of a lane they saw King's Land for the first time—a low pretty house that instantly attracted them. But they could not be sure that this was the house they had come to view. They rode into the village and great was their joy when they had to retrace their steps. The house *was* for sale, it had been empty for some months—an old farmhouse, a magnificent windmill, and some acres of land. Hilaire and Elodie knew their long search for a home had come to an end, and Hilaire was fond of telling intimate friends that they danced a dance of joy together in the large room which at one time had been the village shop.

Hilaire bought the property and settled it on his wife, as those familiar with his verse will recall. One of their neighbours was that extraordinary and remarkable man Wilfrid Blunt. He bred Arab ponies and lived at Crabbit Park in great state; he championed every lost cause from Egypt to Ireland. His friendship both for Hilaire and for Elodie was very close, and they are often mentioned in his *Diaries*.

Bessie again offered to give Hilaire certain pieces of old furniture and some pictures. He answered: "My darling Mother, this is really kind of you. My new house expands and anything of the family is valuable to give my children the atmosphere of their inheritance. I was speaking with John Redmond for the Catholic Schools on the night of my birthday. On Saturday and Sunday I was at Eton. I have only just returned. The session, thank God, is ending! To be in Parliament is of advantage to the family, and it about doubles one's prices, but it is a strain, not so much of work as of a perpetual little fuss. It cuts into one's time enormously. I dined with the new Lord Chancellor the other night. He is very capable. All on my list of proposed magistrates were given the Commission of the Peace—largely because I was moderate in my demands. Good bye, my beloved mother. We shall all be in King's Land please God before the 20th of August. The children will wait till their rooms are finally arranged."

And on September 6th, 1906: ". . . King's Land is now inhabited and one room is respectable. I have yet to arrange my study and finish off the final part, after which it will be in its final form. It has been exceedingly beautiful for the last few days. I am coming over to Slindon and you shall tell me then what day will suit you for your visit. I think you will like it. The only drawback is that there are not quite enough trees round it, but on the other hand the magnificent windmill not only grinds corn but pumps up water and will perhaps give me light later on. Further, there is one of the finest old fireplaces that I know, of the farmhouse kind, in the county. The hot water and baths work well, and the kitchen, which I designed myself and have built onto the house, is admirable. We also have a very fruitful lot of apple trees and the soil is good so that next year we shall have plenty of vegetables. . . .

"Father Gildea of Spanish Place has written me a long letter saying that every step I took on the Education Bill was exactly the step that should have been taken, and that I was the only person in the Commons who understood how to vote. I think he is right. He is one of the very few Catholic priests in the country—or, for the matter of that, Catholic laymen— who knows anything of English politicians or of English society. I don't think it a bad thing for a priest or a layman to know much of evil or corrupt things, such knowledge makes their judgment on a matter of this kind worth having. He is constantly meeting A. J. Balfour, Haldane and men of that stamp in the philosophical societies to which he belongs, and he can test the spirit of the time far better than can the average Catholic in modern England. To my mind it is absolutely certain that unless we manage by dexterity to keep our schools under this Bill, we will lose them for good and all under the next. . . . My new book, *Hills and the Sea,* is out on 4th Oct."

In June, 1907: "Dearest Mamma, when can you come and see King's Land again? It is now thoroughly organized with a chapel and altar for Mass. Oak all around the dining room, a garden laid out and *the drawing-room* properly carpeted and upholstered. Do write to Elodie and suggest a date." Bessie was kept informed of every stage of the house's progress: "When the guest room is habitable, I shall beg you to come and inaugurate its use."

A year later Hilaire wrote: "Dearest Mamma, I am 38 today. I am going to Ponthieu for a day or two, as I am tired. When are you coming to King's Land? The produce of the soil is extraordinary. A profit in vegetables and hay of over £50 when all wages are paid and grazing worth quite another £10 into the bargain. I also grow a great number of various things—aubergines, tomatoes, mushrooms, thyme, sage, flageolets and provençal lentils. My fruit crop makes over 100 lbs. of jam as well as providing eating. It is a fruitful place! The reviews of my novel are lengthy and do it good. But many people object to irony. An historical collection of mine comes out in the autumn. *Marie Antoinette* in the winter."

And again a year later, thanking Bessie for her birthday letter: "My darling Mother, thank you so much for your letter. I am now in my fortieth year and feel the road to be like a country road—leading anywhere. . . . I spoke on fortification yesterday, with no newspaper success but with an admirable if small audience. Balfour came to hear me and was attentive to a degree, also the Prime Minister. It was a minor sort of success. . . . I have got a new horse of a blue colour about which the children were very excited when they heard. He is strong and young and carries my weight, which is a great boon as I have not had sufficient horse riding lately. . . . We have a magnificent rick of hay which we made, and saved in spite of all sorts of difficulties."

And while Hilaire was leading this full and successful life, divided between Parliament, lecturing, writing books, cultivating the soil and building up a permanent home in Sussex, what of his beloved Elodie, who was so soon and so tragically to die?

I have many letters written by Elodie to Bessie and to myself from King's Land. They are happy, cheerful letters. She settled down with the utmost courage to English country life, in spite of what must have been great setbacks to a Californian.

"April, 1908. . . . . We had a heavy fall of snow here in the night, and at four o'clock this morning the world looked more like December than the month of smiles and tears. . . ." Though she had thoroughly enjoyed her life in London, she became so fond of King's Land that I read in a letter of 1908: "I shall not come to town for the Eucharistic Congress." I did, however, manage to persuade her to come to London for the last day of the great Congress, and she watched the procession with us from the balcony of a flat near Westminster Cathedral.

One of her most delightful traits was her enormous capacity for enjoyment of whatever was going on—whether it was a play or, as in this case, a great religious demonstration. Another of her characteristics was great bravery. I recall an occasion when Hilaire was in France and Elodie fell ill. She made no effort to summon Bessie or me at the time, but wrote to Bessie the following day: "Last night I took my crucifix in my hand and made an act of contrition, as it seemed I could drift out anywhere. But thank God I woke up, and now I am well."

Her children were a very great joy to her. Her eldest child Louis was an exceptionally clever boy, and Elodie loved him passionately. I have always remembered her saying to me: "He is not only my child, he is my friend." When came the piteous tidings of his being posted as missing in 1918, I felt thankful his mother was no longer in this world to go through the agony the loss of this boy would have caused her.

Her letters continued to describe all her activities: "December 28, 1908. . . . We had our Christmas tree on Christmas Eve with our household and my ten Sussex boys who make up my Catechism class. Tomorrow we have the children of Shipley with the school-master and his wife, the school-mistress and her father, the assistant school-mistress, the miller and his boy—about eight grown-ups. On Wednesday we have Wilfrid Blunt's grandchildren, the little Lyttons, for another lighting up of the tree, and then comes our Sunday Mass, and then I shall try to take my breath! However, we are all well and have had such a lovely, happy Christmas, thank God.

"The children are well and as happy as birds. Louis is second in his form and his general remarks and conduct were so good that he brought home a huge book of poetry as a sort of extra special prize. Hilary is riding today on the downs with Herbert Fisher of New College."

"King's Land, Feast of the Annunciation. Dearest Grandmamma, many thanks for the dear little shamrock—what a joy it gave my little flock! I have put it away in your envelope with a bunch of violets, a tiny penny bunch that Hilary gave me on March 13th, the day we were with you in Brighton. For on that day eighteen years ago he and I went together to my beloved Californian hills—the hills of Berkeley that look down over the bay of San Francisco and out through the Golden Gate. It was a Californian spring day and the sun was all around us. We have both secretly kept that *fiesta* in our hearts . . . And when Hun told me he was to speak at Brighton and invited me to come, I went to celebrate the date as well as to meet you, and to express my love of Sussex where, please God, I am transplanted—a Californian plant returned to northern skies. After we left you we hurried down to the sea, and we looked out across the grey channel, and we sat for a few minutes on a bench and we thought of that other day so long ago. Then we went to buy shoes and things for the flock. . . .

"Louis came home from school about a fortnight ago. The children adore him and follow him about as a person glorified."

"Dearest Grannie. We all went over to Storrington for Saturday night. It was quite heavenly! There were eight little angels to make their First Holy Communion on Sunday, and we had a lovely High Mass at 8 o'clock and the priests wore their most gorgeous vestments. Hilary and I and the two little girls received the Holy Father's special Pontifical blessing through the Father Prior. Hilary and I and the whole churchful all went to Holy Communion after the little ones, and my one overwhelming emotion was the wonderful unity of the Church, and what a holy Home she is to us weary exiles."

The household that Elodie had to run was a complicated one, and although she had an excellent nurse for the children, she seldom got away from King's Land. By now, too, there was a permanent secretary for Hilaire.

The following letter, written in 1912, is typical of many she wrote at this time: "Dearest Grandmamma, thank you so much for your few lines. I am glad and thankful to say that the flock are all well in spite of the intolerable weather. After our bout of chicken-pox last autumn we have all been well. Hilary is very tired and is making arrangements to have a good long rest. I *kept* him in bed for two days last week in the warmth, and I fed him up and it did him a world of good. Our dear little secretary, Miss Goldsmith, has left us, alas, to be married, and I think Hilary is worrying a bit about her successor. But I am sure the right person will come along. There is of course a great deal to be done, but she will get good wages and has a lot of free time. The difficulty is to get someone quite first rate who will be content with the peace and quiet of Shipley—which are really life to me!"

The letter goes on: "Hilary has built himself in the upper meadow a perfectly heavenly study. The big bow window looks straight at Chanctonbury Ring over the beloved Weald. It is high pitched in its roof and thatched and full of light. We have christened it The Trolls' Hut. When Father Michael comes next he will bless it. It has an enormous down-fire fireplace." This description reminds me of the lines in Hilaire's Sussex poem:

> I will build a house with a deep thatch
>   To shelter me from the cold
> And there shall the Sussex songs be sung
>   And the story of Sussex told.

A word about Elodie's relationship with Bessie—the relationship of a daughter-in-law, one that had been so precious to Bessie long ago. As her letters show, they loved each other truly and deeply and were constantly thinking of small gifts that would please the other. "Dearest Grandmamma, tomorrow will be the Feast of the Purification. I always associate it with your loving friendship with Adelaide Proctor—you told me once that you put a bunch of snowdrops on her coffin. I notice that, however bad the weather, we always have a few of these darling blossoms in the garden; I enclose these few for you."

And: "Dearest Grandmamma, many thanks for the interesting series of Irish portraits that you have sent me. It was so good of you to have got them for me. I have been greatly touched by them and while they have made me proud to see such a shining group of genius in all art and science, still my heart goes out with greater love and greater pride to those unknown and unnamed wanderers who have carried the Faith of God's Church to the limits of the world, and on Sunday mornings when we have the immeasurable blessing of Mass here in King's Land with all our beloved Sussex folk, my mind goes back to those dear graves that lie unknown and unheard of on the hillside in Napa, and in praying for my scattered race I pray that the beloved House of Belloc may be able by God's grace to hold as tenaciously to the Holy Faith as did those exiles and wanderers. How well I know how you love Ireland, and how much she had to do, under God's grace, with bringing you into the true fold! And Hilary's faith—what a blessing it is to see it. And only he and I know *really* how much he has suffered for it. We both went to Holy Communion this morning at Mass in our chapel. It seems to me from my quiet and busy stronghold looking out upon the world that there is nothing worth troubling about in this hard world but the security of the Faith. . . . I am enclosing some little pictures of Soeur Thérèse; if you have them already, perhaps some of the Catholics in Slindon might like to have them."

The chapel in King's Land was a source of great joy to Elodie. "I find that people from the outlying districts are beginning to come to Mass here—this is a great blessing to many who before had to walk five or six miles in all weathers."

There is no need to point out what Elodie's religion meant to her: it shines like a brilliant star through all her letters and all her life. So the following astonishing occurrence at King's Land in 1912 was no surprise. Both she and Hilaire had a devotion to Saint Thérèse of Lisieux before the young nun was even beatified, and Elodie sent the following account of the occurrence to the priest in charge of Thérèse's cause:

"It would be an impossibility to make a list of the favours

that dear Child of God has showered upon us—millions of tiny miracles, misunderstandings cleared up, trying complications smoothed out, hard hearts touched. But I could not begin to tell you what she has done ever since, in a sort of miraculous way, I found first knowledge of her. May God bless her, and may we soon have her 'on our Altars!' All our children pray for her Beatification every day. I have taught them that this is all we can do for her who has done so much for us. . . . We have a little New Forest pony who had a violent attack of double pneumonia. The groom and the veterinary surgeon stayed up with him one whole night, and in the morning he was no better. He was trembling and quivering all over and groaning with pain as he struggled for breath. His poor little head was hanging quite down between his fore feet. I have never seen anything quite so hopeless. I went out of the stable to where Eleanor and Elizabeth were standing in silence and grief and said to them: 'The pony is dying, pray quickly to the Little Flower.' I recited some Hail Marys and went in again to the little creature; I shall never forget the look of love that he gave me. I kept praying to the Little Flower, and I made the Sign of the Cross three times in the name of the Blessed Trinity on his face. He lifted up his neck and walked two or three steps and held up his head, completely changed. I called to Eleanor to run and get a bit of sugar, to see if I could tempt him to eat it. There was a pail of water for him in the corner and some ground barley in his box. Before Eleanor got back he had walked over to his box and begun to eat his food. This is the exact truth. He was eating and drinking in less than five minutes from the moment that I entered the stable, and in less than one since I prayed to the Little Flower. He is alive today, merry and beloved, but he cannot do any carriage work. He can only run about the lanes with the children riding on him."

When on holiday from the House of Commons, Hilaire did not relax from work. "It has been such a joy to me, this vacation from Parliament," Elodie wrote. "It is really the first time for years that Hilary and I have been together at home in the summer. . . . This is due to Miss Beardsley who works so well with him here." A new secretary had been found. At one time she had worked for me, and I believed she would suit the Belloc household. "Miss Beardsley is here now and at work with Hun on his new book. She is such a dear soul, it is a joy to me to have her here with us."

When Hilaire left Parliament, deciding not to stand at the next General Election, his work was not diminished. "Dearest Mamma, I have such an enormous pressure of work that I am only answering now. Of course public opinion is with me, but I do not think it will have any avenues of expression yet. I think it is wise so to have arranged it that I leave under a definite plan and with a definite policy. As a matter of fact, being out of the House of Commons for a little time is an advantage, I think, for I have an enormous amount of work ordered, and income, ultimately, is the important thing. I will write when I have a moment's leisure." He had moved sharply into his politically Independent position.

"Dearest Mamma, very shortly you shall have a copy of my new book all about Sussex called *The Four Men*. It is the story of a walk taken through the county with four men nine years ago, and it has plenty of nice pictures. Nelson & Co. are bringing it out and they are going to charge only 2/- for it, which I am glad of as they have paid me well beforehand, and they are very good at publishing a cheap book. It means quite twenty times the readers that a five or six shilling book has. It is in the manner of *The Path to Rome*. . . . When I was in London the day before yesterday I heard all about the Parliamentary situation. They are in a very dreadful mess. It must come, I think, to an Independent Party of Reformers soon, as I have always wanted, but the trouble is that the formation of such a Party would need a great deal of money."

"King's Land, November 30th, 1912. My beloved Mother, all is well and I am taking a rest. I have put by a sum, I hope, to take things easy for a few weeks and my books are done. I will take an early opportunity of seeing you. I have just been for a long walk for the first time for very many months, seeing my children to a party. I have also greatly admired the downs from the weald. They were magnificent under the night sky which was frosty. . . . I lunched in company with Bonar Law the other day who said he thought there would be an election in a month. The talk in the newspapers about my leading a new Party is all nonsense—it wants more money than will or can possibly be furnished. There is no other news except that my work is full and well paid and that the American market is beginning to rise. . . ."

It was now that Hilaire—as if he had not enough to do— started a paper, largely political, called *The Eye-Witness*. It caused a great stir, and it made clear his belief in Germany's warlike intentions. "Thank you so much, darling Mamma, for your letter. I lunched with Ian Hamilton the other day and he got interested in *Eye-Witness* which he takes in. Do you get it regularly? There was a chance of war last Tuesday but the English Government backed down. I think it was a pity. I think if they had stood out the Germans would have left Agadir. Has Mary Swainson shown you a photograph of the *bust* she made of me? It is exceedingly good, quite separate from most modern work in its economy of detail."

Even his holidays were strenuous. This letter was written in December 1912: "My darling Mother, did I tell you I had been to Silchester? It is a most amazing sight. The amphitheatre is still discernible and quite high, though the stones are

covered by earth and the city walls remain—a huge place!
. . . . The next day I galloped for hours in the New Forest,
a very welcome holiday. . . . Last week a friend and I followed the Roman Road to Old Sarum for miles. . . . Did I
tell you that my book on Stane Street is to be out soon? It is
finely illustrated. . . . *The Century Magazine* are asking me
for 12 articles on the Revolution at £60 each, which is good
pay, is it not? They will afterwards publish it as a book, but
in that I do not expect much though my books are beginning
to sell in America. I have asked Novellos to send you two
copies of my song. It is the first song I have ever published
and I composed both words and tune."

Added to these things, Hilaire often accepted invitations to
speak for Catholic organizations. Thus in October, 1913, he
went to Dublin to speak for the Catholic Truth Society of
Ireland. Elodie did not accompany him though she must have
wanted to do so. I fear she was already feeling below her usual
standard of health.

My brother, devoted though he was to Elodie—and she was
much in his thoughts wherever he happened to be—did not
realize she was delicate. He had seldom known illness. He
naturally could not remember his father's death. When
Elodie fell ill from what proved to be her last illness, he so
little realized her condition, that he was making arrangements
to take her to Italy. He wrote to my mother, "being in the sun
will make her well again." But in December it became obvious to Hilaire that the illness was one which the sun alone
would not cure, though he had absolutely no suspicion of its
fatal nature. He wrote to Bessie and asked her to drive the
fifteen miles between Slindon and King's Land as he was
worried about Elodie. Bessie, who shared the prejudice of her
generation against talking about health, told me nothing of
this visit.

On January 2nd, 1914, he wrote to Bessie saying that a doctor whom Elodie liked and who, I believe, lived in Chelsea, was coming twice a week from London. On January 8th he wrote: "Elodie is appreciably better and the doctor was relieved by the change. I will tell you regularly how things go. She is getting regular sleep now. . . . My great object is, of course, to move her to some warmer place, but the doctor tells me that it will be still a good time before I can do that. . . . I am thinking of going on Sunday to Arundel with the children. It lightens the work to get them out of the house. If I go to Arundel for High Mass, could anyone drive you over?"

"Jan 18th. Dearest Mamma, the only news is that things go up and down. She had two bad nights and consequent neuritis which gave great pain. Then she had two good nights again and it passed. I had such heavy engagements when I went to town that I failed to see Mary, much to my regret. The children were so happy at meeting you the other day and constantly talk about it. Strong as the wind was, and cold, we all sailed out to sea. Peter was a little frightened at first of the waves, but soon got used to it. We then had tea at Worthing and came home in the motor."

Then came the last letter of all, two day's before Elodie died. "Jan 31st. . . . Yesterday Elodie was very ill. I had the children home. The priest came, and for all the morning she was in grave danger. But the doctor coming in the afternoon somewhat reassured me, and he comes again today. Meanwhile things have gone a little better. She suffers less pain, and is more quiet, and she *was* pleased when she saw Louis again! She slept more in the day than in the night, and her pulse is more regular. I am having many Masses said."

Elodie died on February 2nd, 1914, the Feast of the Purification. Hilaire wired the news to his mother, adding: "I shall need all your help."

I was staying with friends near Windsor when I was handed a telegram from Hilaire saying: "My beloved Elodie died to-day." I have never had so terrible, so painfully sudden a shock. I was in a beautiful garden when I opened the telegram, and I recall every moment of the hours that followed. I met Bessie at Horsham that evening and we arrived together at King's Land. I remember the appearance of the desolate house and the little children sitting around, stunned by the fearful misfortune that had just befallen them.

Hilaire had Elodie's coffin moved to the room they had recently added to the house. There she lay for many hours while the village people came to pray—for Elodie, after over seven years at King's Land, had made friends with people of every walk of life in the neighbourhood.

I remember at the funeral the curious sight of Wilfrid Blunt driving his phaeton and forcing his Arab horses with great difficulty to keep to walking pace.

When Elodie died, the five children ranged in age from Louis, who was sixteen, to Peter who was nine. Thereafter Hilaire seldom went to visit a country-house in the school holidays without taking some, or all, of his children with him. His devoted friends—and no man of his time had more devoted friends—both men and women, did their best for him, and some advised him to leave King's Land. But he had become exceedingly fond of his home—the home that Elodie and he had created—and he lived there for the rest of his days. Work, travel, the love of his children, and the affection that bound mother and son together until her death, filled his life.

His grief at this time finds expression in these noble words from *The Cruise of the Nona:* "The sea has taken me to itself whenever I sought it and has given me relief from men. It has rendered remote the cares and wastes of the land, for of all creatures that move and breathe upon the earth we of mankind are the fullest of sorrow. But the sea shall comfort us, and perpetually show us new things that assure us. It is the common sacrament of the world. May it be to others what it has been to me."

This book, describing as it does Hilaire's youth and the two women in his life—his mother and his wife—now inevitably draws to a close. When the children had returned to school after Elodie's death, to our relief he decided to travel in Europe, and I shall conclude this family record with the following letter from him which came during one of my mother's constant visits to my house in London: "My beloved Mamma, I shall call on you in Barton Street at *3.30* tomorrow, Monday, before starting for Rome, and get your blessing as I did all those years ago in New York when I went off on the second of my three journeys. Your dutiful and devoted son, Hilaire."